6

Math for the Gifted Student
Challenging Activities for the Advanced Learner

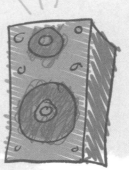

Written by **Danielle Denega**
Illustrations by **Dave Garbot**

An imprint of Sterling Children's Books

FLASH KIDS, STERLING, and the distinctive Sterling logo are registered trademarks of
Sterling Publishing Co., Inc.

Published by Sterling Publishing Co., Inc.
387 Park Avenue South, New York, NY 10016
Text and illustrations © 2005 by Flash Kids
Distributed in Canada by Sterling Publishing
c/o Canadian Manda Group, 165 Dufferin Street
Toronto, Ontario, Canada M6K 3H6
Distributed in the United Kingdom by GMC Distribution Services
Castle Place, 166 High Street, Lewes, East Sussex, England BN7 1XU
Distributed in Australia by Capricorn Link (Australia) Pty. Ltd.
P.O. Box 704, Windsor, NSW 2756, Australia

Sterling ISBN 978-1-4114-3438-7

Manufactured in Canada

Lot #:
2   4   6   8   10   9   7   5   3
06/13

For information about custom editions, special sales, premium and
corporate purchases, please contact Sterling Special Sales
Department at 800-805-5489 or specialsales@sterlingpublishing.com.

Cover image © Thomas Northcut/Getty Images
Cover design and production by Mada Design, Inc.

If you find that your child is unchallenged

by traditional workbooks and math practice drills, this workbook will provide the stimulation your student has been looking for. This workbook contains much more than typical sixth-grade drill pages and questions; it does not rely on the assumption that a gifted sixth grader simply requires seventh-grade work. The logic-based activities cover the national math standards for sixth grade while also providing kids with a chance to grow and challenge themselves beyond the work they do in the regular classroom. This workbook covers the curriculum areas of algebra, statistics, measurement, geometry, probability, estimation, and problem solving.

Encourage your student to use models or scrap paper to work out problems or to help him or her work through more difficult activities. Allow your student to skip around and do activities that interest him or her. The activities in the book encourage independent thinking and stimulate creativity. Your student can check his or her answers by using the answer key at the end of the book.

By utilizing this workbook series, you are providing your gifted learner an opportunity to experience scholastic achievement at an advanced level, thereby fostering confidence and an increased desire to learn.

Jurassic Numbers

Write the numeral described in each fossilized fact below.

1. The Cretaceous period ended 65.5 million years ago. _____

2. The Jurassic period began 208 million years ago. _____

3. The Triassic period began 248 million years ago. _____

4. The Cretaceous period began 145.5 million years ago. _____

5. The *Brachiosaurus* could have weighed one hundred thirty thousand pounds.

_____

6. Some scientists estimate that earth is 4.6 billion years old. _____

7. The oldest rocks currently known are believed to be 3.8 billion years old.

_____

8. The Archean eon ended 2.5 billion years ago. _____

9. The Precambrian era began 4.6 billion years ago.

_____

10. The Ordovician period ended 443 million years ago.

_____

11. The Quaternary period began 1.8 million years ago. _____

12. The Carboniferous period began 360 million years ago. _____

Painting Problems!

Jesse Gray had some trouble mixing paint for the customers in his father's hardware store. His father left him instructions. The mixes that Jesse created appear below. Use = or ≠ signs to express whether Jesse's proportions were correct.

Please mix one gallon each of the following paints:

1. Canary yellow = 9 parts lemon yellow : 1 part white
2. Baby blue = 1 part sky blue : 7 parts white
3. Creamsicle = 3 parts orange : 2 parts white
4. Sage = 5 parts evergreen : 4 parts white
5. Sandy shores = 9 parts brown : 14 parts white
6. Lavender = 3 parts purple : 5 parts white
7. Linen = 5 parts cream : 6 parts white
8. Barn red = 7 parts brick red : 2 parts white
9. Elephant gray = 1 part black : 4 parts white
10. Meadow = 12 parts evergreen : 13 parts lemon yellow
11. Indigo = 7 parts purple : 8 parts blue
12. Melon = 2 parts orange : 3 parts lemon yellow

	Jesse's mix		Correct mix		Jesse's mix		Correct mix
1.	$\dfrac{27}{3}$	_____	$\dfrac{9}{1}$	7.	$\dfrac{55}{60}$	_____	$\dfrac{5}{6}$
2.	$\dfrac{3}{28}$	_____	$\dfrac{1}{7}$	8.	$\dfrac{217}{62}$	_____	$\dfrac{7}{2}$
3.	$\dfrac{27}{18}$	_____	$\dfrac{3}{2}$	9.	$\dfrac{500}{20,000}$	_____	$\dfrac{1}{4}$
4.	$\dfrac{20}{12}$	_____	$\dfrac{5}{4}$	10.	$\dfrac{14}{19}$	_____	$\dfrac{12}{13}$
5.	$\dfrac{36}{42}$	_____	$\dfrac{9}{14}$	11.	$\dfrac{11}{13}$	_____	$\dfrac{7}{8}$
6.	$\dfrac{63}{105}$	_____	$\dfrac{3}{5}$	12.	$\dfrac{88}{132}$	_____	$\dfrac{2}{3}$

On Common Ground

Find the least common multiple for the following pairs of numbers.

1. 4 and 5   _____

2. 12 and 16   _____

3. 6 and 7   _____

4. 6 and 9   _____

5. 19 and 5   _____

6. 2 and 6   _____

Find the greatest common factor for the following pairs of numbers.

7. 8 and 20   _____

8. 12 and 36   _____

9. 17 and 85   _____

10. 36 and 48   _____

11. 22 and 121   _____

12. 18 and 99   _____

Doing Decimals

Write the amount that is double each number below.

1. 784,372.15   _____

2. 651,306.09   _____

3. 9,899.99   _____

4. −5,577.55   _____

Calculate the value of each number below to the second power.

5. 49.7   _____

6. −0.23   _____

7. 4.44   _____

8. 191.1   _____

Calculate the amount that is 15 percent higher than each number below.

9. 15.19   _____

10. 22.2   _____

11. 6.3   _____

12. 500.1   _____

Nifty Gift!

Janie Generous enjoys giving generously. Whenever she visits friends and family, she brings gifts. Use your knowledge of the distributive property to evaluate the questions below. Write each problem as a numeric equation and provide the answer.

1. Janie visits her 2 cousins and their 9 children. She gives 4 gifts to each person. How many gifts does she bring? _____

2. Janie visits 3 friends and their 2 neighbors. She gives 2 gifts to each person. How many gifts does she bring? _____

3. Janie visits her grandmother and her 7 great-aunts. She gives 3 gifts to each person. How many gifts does she bring? _____

4. Janie visits her 2 doctors and the nurse. She gives 4 gifts to each person. How many gifts does she bring? _____

5. Janie visits her aunt Mabel, her uncle Henry, and her 5 second cousins. She gives 8 gifts to each person. How many gifts does she bring? _____

6. Janie visits her 2 stepbrothers and 4 stepsisters. She gives 13 gifts to each person. How many gifts does she bring? _____

7. Janie visits her 3 college roommates and their 3 husbands. She gives 11 gifts to each person. How many gifts does she bring? _____

8. Janie visits her sister, her brother-in-law, her 6 nephews, and her 2 nieces. She gives 4 gifts to each person. How many gifts does she bring? _____

9. Janie visits her dogs' 2 veterinarians and their 4 vet techs. She gives 2 gifts to each person. How many gifts does she bring? _____

10. Janie visits her daughter's 3 teachers and their 14 students. She gives 3 gifts to each person. How many gifts does she bring? _____

11. Janie visits her mother and father. She gives 19 gifts to each person. How many gifts does she bring? _____

12. Janie received a thank-you note from each of her gift recipients. How many thank-you notes did she receive? _____

Lunchtime!

Use the information provided to answer the questions below. Show your answers in lowest terms.

Every student eats lunch in the school cafeteria. There are 7 different meals: chicken tacos, meat lasagna, fish sticks, grilled cheese, vegetarian chili, cheese pizza, and baked chicken. Each day a different meal is served. There are 300 trays at the cafeteria. Of the trays, 180 are blue and 120 are red.

1. Neal likes only pizza. What is the probability that pizza will be served today? _____

2. Emma eats only chicken dishes. What is the probability that today's lunch will contain chicken?

_____

3. Nathan eats no meat or chicken, but he does eat fish. What is the probability that a meal Nathan would eat will be served for lunch today? _____

4. Stella brings her lunch on the days when her sister Emma isn't going to buy the school lunch. What is the probability that Stella brought her lunch? _____

5. What is the probability that Charlie will pick a red tray? _____

6. What is the probability that Kurt will pick a blue tray? _____

7. Students are scheduled to eat lunch at 11:45, 12:15, 12:45, or 1:15. What is the probability that Kit's best friend will have the same lunch period that she does? _____

8. Matt brings the same lunch every day: turkey on wheat. What is the probability that he will bring turkey on wheat tomorrow? _____

Angling for Angles

Identify whether each angle below is a *straight* angle, a *right* angle, an *acute* angle, or an *obtuse* angle.

1. 30°   _____

2. 60°   _____

3. 100°   _____

4. 90°   _____

5. 180°   _____

6. 150°   _____

7. 40°   _____

8. 160°   _____

9. 179°   _____

10. 80°   _____

Answer the following questions about angles.

11. Name three of the angles above that could form an acute triangle.

_____

12. Name three of the angles above that could form a right triangle.

_____

Negative Thinking

Solve the following equations involving negative numbers.

1. −2,593 + −1,339   _____

2. −681 + 615   _____

3. −2,222 + −1,458   _____

4. −12 × 57   _____

5. −789 × −923   _____

6. −(14)^2 + 2   _____

7. −6^3 − 16   _____

8. −4n + 7 = 39   _____

9. −4(n + 7) = 0   _____

10. −$\frac{3}{4}$ ÷ 5   _____

11. −$\frac{2}{3}$ ÷ −$\frac{3}{2}$ _____

12. −1,204 ÷ −16   _____

Tag Sale!

Tim and Tina Sellers had a weekend-long tag sale. Today is the last day of the sale and everything must go.
The Sellers are offering everything at a discount according to the chart below.
Use the chart to determine the sale price of the items below.

ONE-DAY TAG SALE!

Red sticker → 15% Off
Yellow sticker → 20% Off
Blue sticker → 25% Off
Green Sticker → 50% Off
Orange sticker → 75% Off

1. Fifteen books are priced at $.50 each. They all have yellow stickers. _____

2. Two CDs are priced at $2 each. They both have red stickers. _____

3. A giant stuffed elephant is $1.50. It has a green sticker. _____

4. A bundle of videotapes is $1. It has an orange sticker. _____

5. A picture frame that says "My Nana Rocks" is $.80. It has a yellow sticker. _____

6. A ten-speed bicycle with a wicker basket is $12. It has a blue sticker. _____

7. A poster that pictures furry kittens is $2. It has an orange sticker. _____

8. A kit for growing sea monkeys is $2.90. It has a green sticker. _____

9. A bag of Zapping Zed action figures is $3.20. It has a red sticker. _____

10. A leopard print dog collar with matching leash is $4.60. It has a blue sticker. _____

11. A platter that says "Dad's Grill: Always Open" is $1.50. It has a yellow sticker. _____

12. How much did the Sellers earn from the above items? _____

Not Like the Others

Circle the item in each row that is not equal to the others.

1. $\frac{17}{51}$	$\frac{6}{18}$	$\frac{89}{267}$	$\frac{43}{172}$
2. $\frac{1}{8}$	12.5%	4:48	0.125
3. $28\sqrt{49}$	390	196	$\frac{588}{3}$
4. 1 cup	$\frac{1}{12}$ gallon	$\frac{1}{2}$ pint	16 tablespoons
5. $\frac{243}{9}$	3^3	$\frac{54}{2}$	64
6. 44:8	10.5	$\frac{11}{2}$	550%
7. 0.8125	$\frac{52}{64}$	108	$8\frac{6.5}{8}$ %
8. 3:4	64:48	2:1.5	16:12
9. 4.5 m	45 cm	450 cm	4,500 mm
10. $\frac{20}{8}$	4.25	$\frac{34}{8}$	$\frac{12.75}{3}$
11. $93\frac{3}{4}$ %	$\frac{30}{32}$	$\frac{1.875}{2}$	$9\frac{3}{4}$
12. $\frac{3}{4}$ foot	$\frac{1}{5}$ yard	9 inches	0.25 yard

Market Research

Answer the questions below.

1. With your family, determine how much money is spent on groceries each week. _____

2. The chart below represents the average that families spend on groceries.

Size of Family	Annual Expense	Weekly Expense
1	$2,500	$48
2	$4,366	$84
3	$5,228	$101
4	$6,280	$121
5 or more	$6,805	$131

Compare your family's spending to the chart. How does it compare? Explain.

_____

_____

_____

3. If you found that your family is spending more or less than the average family on groceries, what might be some reasons for this discrepancy? _____

_____

_____

_____

Ratio Rodeo

For each set of numbers, write two different ways to express it as a ratio.

1. 3 to 5 _____ _____

2. 1:8 _____ _____

3. $\frac{2}{7}$ _____ _____

4. $\frac{5}{9}$ _____ _____

5. 6:5 _____ _____

6. 3 to 11 _____ _____

Now write each ratio as a fraction in lowest terms.

7. 8 steer to 64 horses _____

8. 24 barrels to 72 poles _____

9. 1 rider to 9 ropes _____

10. *x* cows to *y* calves _____

11. *n* veterinarians to 1 animal _____

12. 7 horses to 2 trainers _____

Bargain Hunters

Krista, Tamika, and Tyler were chosen to help their teacher shop for classroom supplies.
Help them choose the best bargain for each item.

1. Rubber erasers

   a. $0.32 each

   b. box of 24 for $7.44

   c. buy two for $0.90 and get
      one free

2. Pencils

   a. 12 packs of 12 for $17.28

   b. 4 pencils for $0.50

   c. buy a box of 12 for $3.12
      and get one free

3. Chalk

   a. box of eight sticks for $0.64

   b. four packs of 8 sticks for
      $2.72

   c. bulk box of 1 gross for
      $10.80

4. Ballpoint pens

   a. $0.27 each

   b. buy 2 boxes of 12 for $6.84,
      get half off the next box

   c. bulk pack of 100 for $28

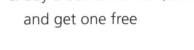

5. Calculators

   a. set of four for $16.92

   b. buy one for $8.45, get one
      free

   c. 10-pack for $43

6. Markers

   a. box of eight for $2.60

   b. bulk pack of 32 for $13.60,
      on sale for 20% off

   c. 12-pack for $4.02

7. Protractors

   a. $0.52 each

   b. box of 24 for $12.36

   c. buy three boxes of four for
      $7.84, get one free

8. Glue sticks

   a. box of 12 with two bonus
      sticks for $11.06

   b. four-pack for $3.08

   c. buy one for $1.64, get one
      free

Counting the Days

Use your knowledge of percentages to answer the questions below.
Assume that it is **not** a leap year. Round your answers to the nearest whole number.

1. What percentage of the year is one week? _____

2. The 30th and 31st days of all months comprise what percentage of the year? _____

3. What percentage of the year occurs on Saturday? Note: January 1 is not Saturday. _____

4. What percentage of the year occurs in September? _____

5. What percentage of the year occurs in a month that begins with "J"? _____

6. What percentage of the year occurs in a month that begins with "A"? _____

7. What percentage of the year occurs in a month that begins with "M"? _____

8. What percentage of the year occurs in a month that ends with "Y"? _____

Raining Cats and Dogs

Use the information provided to fill in the Venn diagrams and answer the questions below.

1. Dr. Katz is a veterinarian. He has 100 clients who have at least one cat or dog. Of his clients, 29 people have cats and 12 people have cats and dogs.

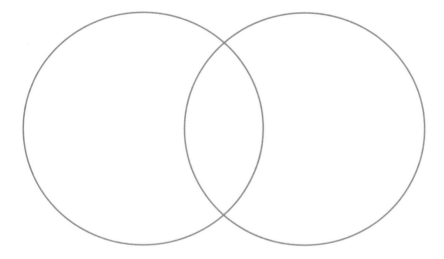

How many people have only dogs? _____

2. A team surveyed 100 zoos that keep lions or tigers. Of the zoos, 55 have lions and 17 have lions and tigers.

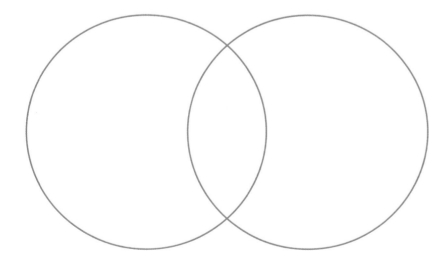

How many zoos have only tigers? _____

Speedy Skater

Speed skater Cole Winter recorded a winning time of 34.70 seconds in the 500-meter event at this year's International Snow Games. Use the information provided to answer the questions below.

1. Give Cole's winning speed as meters per second. Round your answer to one decimal place.

_____

2. If Cole's speed is 2,756 feet per minute, give his speed as miles per hour. Round to the nearest whole number. Show your work.

_____

_____

_____

3. If Cole were to travel at the same speed in the 1,500-meter event as he did for the 500-meter event this year, what would his finish time be? Give your answer as minutes and seconds.

_____

4. At last year's Snow Games, Cole was disappointed with his results in the 500-meter event. His time was 2.75 seconds longer than it was this year. What was his time? _____

5. Give Cole's time from last year's Snow Games as meters per second. Round the figure for meters to one decimal place. _____

6. Who travels faster: Cole or a sprinter who can run a 100-meter race in 12 seconds?

_____

7. Cole's goal is to travel 14.8 meters per second in the 500-meter event. What would his time need to be? Round your answer to two decimal places. _____

8. The world record holder for the 500-meter event traveled at 15.0 meters per second. What was his time? Round your answer to two decimal places. _____

The Factor Reactor

The reactor has blown, and the following numbers have been blasted into their prime factors.
Match each item in column A with its correct prime factorization in column B.

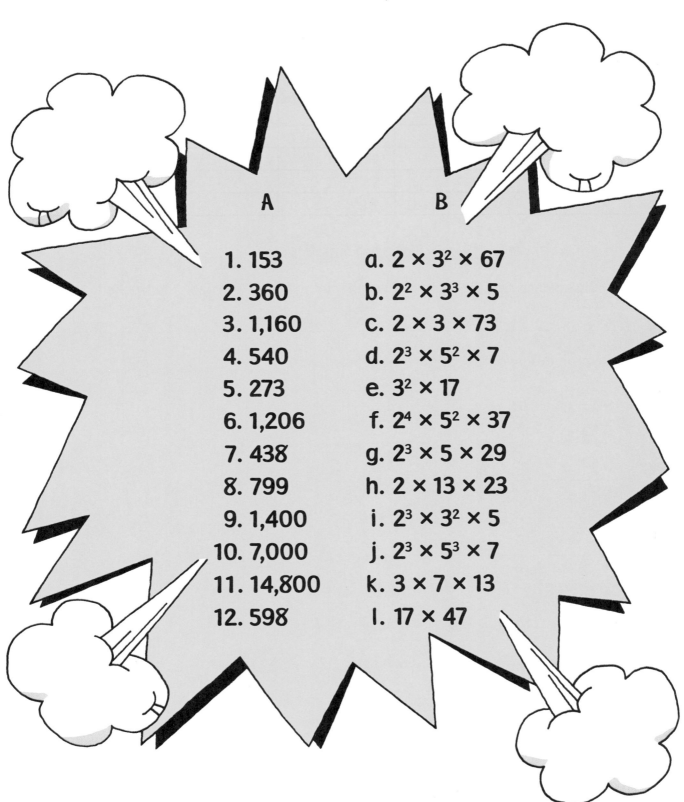

A	B
1. 153	a. $2 \times 3^2 \times 67$
2. 360	b. $2^2 \times 3^3 \times 5$
3. 1,160	c. $2 \times 3 \times 73$
4. 540	d. $2^3 \times 5^2 \times 7$
5. 273	e. $3^2 \times 17$
6. 1,206	f. $2^4 \times 5^2 \times 37$
7. 438	g. $2^3 \times 5 \times 29$
8. 799	h. $2 \times 13 \times 23$
9. 1,400	i. $2^3 \times 3^2 \times 5$
10. 7,000	j. $2^3 \times 5^3 \times 7$
11. 14,800	k. $3 \times 7 \times 13$
12. 598	l. 17×47

Box Office Bonanza

Use the information in the chart to answer the questions below.

WEEKEND ENDING MAY 14

This Week	Last Week	Title	Weekend Gross Theaters	Cumulative Gross	Release Weeks	# of Theaters
1	1	*Hero Hank*	$43,800,000	$394,887,000	5	4,215
2	–	*One Mistake*	$42,250,000	$42,250,000	1	3,760
3	2	*My Day*	$16,300,000	$62,966,000	2	3,095
4	3	*Tara's Sister*	$13,121,000	$87,975,000	3	3,062
5	4	*Princess Lake*	$6,875,000	$73,140,000	2	2,285

1. What was the total weekend gross for the top 5 movies? _____

2. What was the average number of dollars per theater that *My Day* made the weekend of May 14?

_____

3. Rank the films in descending order of cumulative gross.

_____

_____

_____

_____

_____

4. What is the average number of weeks the top 5 movies have been released? _____

5. What is *Hero Hank's* average gross revenue per week of release? _____

6. How much money did *Tara's Sister* gross in its first 2 weeks of release? _____

7. How much money did *One Mistake* gross the weekend ending May 7? Explain.

_____

8. What is the average cumulative gross for the weekend's top 5 films? _____

Occupation Confusion

Use the information in the box to determine each person's job.

> Ms. Bennet, Mr. Kearney, Ms. March, and Mr. Danube are neighbors. One of them is an engineer, one of them is a doctor, one of them is a lawyer, and one of them is a writer. Ms. Bennet lives between the engineer and the doctor. Mr. Kearney went to college with the lawyer and the writer. Ms. March had the lawyer give her contract advice. Mr. Danube had lunch with the lawyer and the doctor. Mr. Kearney and Ms. March are not engineers.

1. Ms. Bennet is _____.

2. Mr. Kearney is _____.

3. Ms. March is _____.

4. Mr. Danube is _____.

Temperature Trends

Use the chart to answer the questions that follow.

AVERAGE TEMPERATURES

Month	San Antonio, TX	Iowa City, IA
January	62	30
February	67	37
March	74	49
April	80	63
May	86	75
June	91	84
July	95	88
August	95	85
September	90	78
October	82	66
November	71	48
December	64	34

1. Draw a bar graph that shows the average monthly temperatures for San Antonio, Texas.

2. Between which months does the temperature change the most in San Antonio?

_____

3. Between which months does the temperature change the least in San Antonio?

_____

4. Draw a bar graph that shows the average monthly temperatures for Iowa City, Iowa.

5. Between which months does the temperature change the most in Iowa City?

_____

6. Between which months does the temperature change the least in Iowa City?

_____

7. During which month(s) is the average temperature in San Antonio closest to the average temperature in Iowa City?

_____

8. During which month(s) is the average temperature of both cities furthest apart?

_____

Spelling Success

Rosa has to learn the 14 words listed for her spelling quiz. Use Rosa's spelling list to answer the questions. Round your answers to the nearest whole number.

Spelling List

amphibian	inflatable	simile
boycott	interchangeable	skiing
calendar	judgment	sluggish
despised	misspell	tomorrow
independence	persuasion	

1. What percentage of words starts with *i*? _____

2. What percentage of words ends with *t*? _____

3. What percentage of vowels found in the spelling list is *o?* _____

4. What percentage of the words contains at least one double letter pair? (Example: *mm* or *ee*)

_____

5. What percentage of all the letters of the alphabet is included somewhere on this word list?

_____

6. How much longer is the longest word than the shortest word? Express your answer as a percentage. _____

7. Rosa scored a 93% on her spelling quiz. During the quiz, she had to spell each of the words on the list once. How many questions did she get correct? _____

8. Rosa misspelled a word that contains the 10th letter of the alphabet. Which word is it?

_____

School Days, Cool Days

Mrs. Miller's science class at Snowville Middle School tracked the temperature outside their school for a week in January. Use the information provided to answer the questions below.

1. The temperature was −3°F on Monday morning. By noon, the temperature had risen by 10 degrees. What was the temperature? _____

2. By 3:30 PM on Monday, the temperature dropped 2 degrees. What was the temperature?

_____

3. Tuesday brought blustery wind and was terribly cold. The students recorded a temperature that was 5 degrees colder than it had been on Monday morning. What was the temperature?

_____

4. On Wednesday morning, the temperature was 0°F. It rose 9 degrees later in the day. What was the temperature? _____

5. The temperature at noon on Thursday was three degrees colder than the temperature on Monday morning. What was the temperature? _____

6. By the end of the day on Friday, the temperature was twice as warm as it had been at 3:30 on Monday. What was the temperature? _____

7. Draw a number line that shows all of the temperatures the students recorded.

8. School is closed if the temperature falls below −23°C. How many times was school closed the week the temperatures were recorded? _____

Round Up!

Use rounding to answer the questions below.

1. What is 767 rounded to the nearest hundred? _____

2. What is 14,497 rounded to the nearest thousand? _____

3. What is 19,712,576 rounded to the nearest million? _____

Now solve the following equations. Round your answers as indicated.

4. $\frac{1}{2}(5^2 + 9)$. Round your answer to the nearest ten. _____

5. $9^3 + 5^3$. Round your answer to the nearest thousand. _____

6. 1,500,725 ÷ 5. Round your answer to the nearest hundred thousand. _____

7. 0.34 + 0.39. Round your answer to the nearest tenth. _____

8. $4\frac{1}{4} \times \frac{1}{2}$. Round your answer to the nearest one. _____

Use estimation to answer the following questions. (Hint: use rounded numbers when estimating.)

9. Mrs. Perk buys a cup of coffee every day for $0.93. About how much money does she spend on coffee each week? _____

10. Rose runs 28 minutes a day, 4 days a week. About how many minutes does she run each week?

_____

11. Kavita bought a sweater for $19.50, socks for $1.89, and a pair of jeans for $30.19. About how much did she spend? _____

12. Matteo's cell phone bill was $20.92 in September, $34.87 in October, and $29.76 in November. About how much did he pay during those three months? _____

13. The Davis family spends $28.64 on pizza each month. About how much do they spend on pizza in a year? _____

14. Glenda writes in her journal each night for 38 minutes. About how many minutes does she write in her journal each week? _____

15. Mrs. Balk spends $7.75 at the laundromat every Saturday. About how much does she spend at the laundromat each month? _____

16. Belinda watches cartoons for 22 minutes every morning. About how many minutes does she watch cartoons in a month? _____

Bake Sale

The football team is holding a bake sale to raise money for new uniforms.
Use the information provided to answer the questions below.

1. Brownies cost $0.35 each. How much do 2 dozen cost? _____

2. Cupcakes are 3 for $1.80. How much do 2 cost? _____

3. A plate of a dozen cookies is $1.95. How much do 60 cookies cost? _____

4. A Bundt cake costs $11.50. Some of the Bundt cakes were cut into 14 slices. Each slice costs
$0.85. Which will raise more money: selling a cake or selling 14 slices of cake? _____

5. A slice of Roxie's apple pie costs $1.15. There are 8 slices cut from each pie. Pie slices earned
$63.25 for the bake sale. How many pies were needed to sell this much? _____

6. Which costs more: 5 brownies or 2 slices of Bundt cake? _____

7. Which costs more: 5 slices of apple pie or 6 slices of Bundt cake?

_____

8. During the last hour of the bake sale, all baked goods are 30% off. How much would it cost to
buy 12 cookies, 3 brownies, 1 cupcake, and 2 slices of apple pie after the discount? _____

Camp Kitchen Raid

Answer the tasty questions below.

1. The campers made 30 s'mores treats. Josiah ate 3 and Barron ate 3. How many s'mores were eaten by the other 6 campers if they ate equal amounts of s'mores?

   _____

2. Camp Chef Cramer made 3 more cups of chili than Camp Chef Cosby, who made 9 cups of chili. Chef Cramer and Chef Cosby shared their chili with the other 2 chefs at camp. If each chef ate the same amount of chili, how many cups of chili did each chef get? _____

3. Marji ate $14\frac{1}{2}$ silver dollar pancakes at the mess hall this morning. That was $6\frac{1}{2}$ more pancakes than she bet James she could eat. How many pancakes did James think Marji could eat? _____

4. Before his hike, both of Anshu's 32-ounce water bottles were full. At the end of his hike, there were only 7 ounces of water left in total. How much water did Anshu drink during his hike?

   _____

5. Animals raided the camp pantry and got into the cereal. The animals ate 2 packages of Dan's, 3 packages of Viraj's, and 6 packages of Jean-Paul's. The animals ate $\frac{1}{2}$ as much of Todd's cereal as the other campers' combined. How much of Todd's cereal did the animals eat?

   _____

6. Jon and Risa drank the same number of cups of bug juice. Together, this was 3 fewer than twice what Jackie drank. Jackie drank 5 cups. How many cups of bug juice did Jon and Risa each drink?

   _____

Field Goal Fury

Use the information in the chart to answer the questions below.

FOOTBALL'S LEADING KICKERS

Kicker	Field Goals Made	Field Goals Attempted
1	29	32
2	24	29
3	25	28
4	28	33
5	24	28
6	31	33
7	29	34
8	24	31

1. What was the mean number of field goals made by the eight kickers? _____

2. What was the median number of field goals made? _____

3. What was the mode number of field goals made? _____

4. What was the mean number of field goals attempted but not made? _____

5. Which kicker has the highest ratio of kicks made to kicks attempted? _____

6. Which kicker has the lowest ratio of kicks made to kicks attempted? _____

7. Field goals are worth three points. How many points did kickers 2, 3, and 6 score combined?

_____

8. Kicker 6 earned a total of 139 points between field goals and extra point kicks made. Extra point kicks are worth one point each. How many extra point kicks did he make? _____

Valley of the Kings

Ancient Egyptian pharaohs were buried in pyramids. Calculate the volume of the following pyramids.

1. $h = 15$ ft
$b = 25$ ft

_____

2. $h = 90$ ft
$b = 118$ ft

_____

3. $h = 38$ ft
$b = 57$ ft

_____

4. $h = 27$ ft
$b = 40$ ft

_____

5. $h = 117$ ft
$b = 145$ ft

_____

6. $h = 41$ ft
$b = 51$ ft

_____

7. $h = 45$ ft
$b = 57$ ft

_____

8. $h = 18$ ft
$b = 27$ ft

_____

Text Me

Serena took a survey of the number of text messages her friends sent last month.
Use the chart to answer the questions below.

Name	Number of Text Messages Sent
Abraham	2
Bella	12
Rico	3
Ava	18
Wanda	7
Gabriela	12
Paula	5
Caitlyn	159
Jack	9
Will	12
Mary	13

1. What is the mean number of text messages sent by the group? Round your answer to the nearest whole number. _____

2. What is the mode number of text messages sent by the group? _____

3. What is the median number of text messages sent by the group? _____

4. Why are the median and mean so different? Which one offers Serena a more accurate picture of how often her friends send text messages? Explain. _____

_____

_____

_____

5. If you exclude Caitlyn, what is the mean? _____

6. What is the mean number of text messages sent by the boys? _____

7. What is the mean number of text messages sent by the girls? _____

8. What is the mean for the girls if you exclude Caitlyn? _____

Star Slugger

The Mayville Manatees just signed Morris Better, a switch hitter.
Use the chart to answer the following questions about Better's stats.

PLAYER: MORRIS BETTER			
Situation Splits	AVG	AB	H
Day	0.297	101	30
Night		117	33

Key: AVG = average; AB = at bats; H = hits

1. The batter's average is the ratio of hits to at bats. What is Better's average for night games?

   _____

2. Has Better had more at bats during day games or night games? _____

3. What is Better's average for day and night games combined? _____

4. How many hits has Better had this season? _____

5. Better scored two runs in last night's winning game. The final score was 9 to 3. What percentage of his team's runs did Better score? Round your answer to the nearest whole number. _____

6. The Manatees are playing a doubleheader. There will be one game this afternoon and one game tonight. Better can play in only one of those games. Based on his batting average, which one should he play and why? _____

   _____

   _____

7. If Better has three at bats and one hit in the next day game, what would be his new day average for the season? _____

8. Better has hit 4 home runs this season. What percentage of his total hits were home runs? Round your answer to the nearest whole number. _____

35

Coin Conundrum

Use the chart and your knowledge of money to answer the questions below.

Coin	Diameter	Weight
Penny	19 mm	2.5 grams
Nickel	21 mm	5 grams
Dime	18 mm	2.3 grams

1. Determine the circumference of a penny. _____

2. Determine the area of a penny. _____

3. A row of pennies set end to end is 1.52 meters long. How many pennies are there? _____

4. A group of pennies weighs 2,500 kilograms. How many pennies are there? _____

5. Determine the circumference of a nickel. _____

6. Determine the area of a nickel. _____

7. A row of nickels set end to end is 35.7 centimeters long. How many nickels are there? _____

8. A group of nickels is worth $4.75. How much do they weigh? _____

9. Determine the circumference of a dime. _____

10. Determine the area of a dime. _____

11. A group of dimes weighs 172.5 grams. How many dimes are there? _____

12. A stack of dimes weighs 345 grams. How much money is there in the stack? _____

13. How much more money is 138 grams of dimes than 275 grams of nickels? _____

14. Measure the diameter of a quarter and record it here. _____

15. Determine the circumference of a quarter. _____

16. Determine the area of a quarter. _____

Mysterious Shape

Answer the questions below.

1. Draw a quadrilateral with equal sides of 4 inches and no angles that equal 90°.

2. What is the figure in question 1 called? _____

3. Draw a quadrilateral with four 90° angles. Two sides have a length of 3 inches. The other 2 sides have a length of 2 inches.

4. What is the figure in question 3 called? _____

5. Draw a quadrilateral with four 90° angles. All sides are 4 inches.

6. What is the figure in question 5 called? _____

7. Draw a quadrilateral with 1 pair of parallel sides. There are no 90° angles. Sides are the following lengths: the top is 6 inches; the bottom is 11 inches; the left side is 5.9 inches; the right side is 5.9 inches.

8. What is the figure in question 7 called? _____

A Penny Saved

Choose the best answer for the following questions about saving money.

1. Penny Moneybags has $25. Which of the following choices will help Penny's money grow the most?

    a. Penny's brother, Nickel Moneybags, offered to sell Penny his stamp collection for $25. The stamp collection is worth $25.98.

    b. Penny could put her $25 in her saving account for one year. The account earns 5% interest.

    c. Penny's father, George Washington Moneybags, offered to put Penny's $25 into his savings account for one year. Her money would earn 2 cents in interest every week.

    d. Penny could loan the $25 to her friend, who offered to pay her back $26 after one year.

2. Which will be worth more after one year:

    a. $27,000 in an account that earns interest at a rate of 5% a year.

    b. $21,000 in an account that earns interest at a rate of 13% a year.

    c. $24,000 in an account that earns interest at a rate of 9% a year.

    d. $29,000 in an account that earns interest at a rate of 3% a year.

3. Which is worth the most:

    a. $2.76
    b. 7 quarters, 5 dimes, eight nickels, and a penny
    c. 3 quarters, 15 dimes, two nickels, and fifteen pennies
    d. $1.98

4. George Washington Moneybags gave his children, Penny and Nickel, a choice about how much allowance they would receive. Which is the best choice?

    a. $1 a week
    b. $4.50 a month
    c. $0.10 a day
    d. $50 a year

Clearance Sale

Dave-Mart, the discount department store, is having a clearance sale. Using the information below, calculate the total price of the items each person has purchased. There is no tax on clothing and accessory items under $150.

1. Dinah bought a $30 sweater and a $6 necklace. _____

2. Jim bought a $15 belt. _____

3. Josie bought a $45 dress and a $35 pair of boots. _____

4. Damian bought a $50 pair of sneakers and an $8 pack of socks. _____

5. Mary-Kate bought two $35 pairs of jeans and a $20 blouse. _____

6. Hugo bought a $40 pair of jeans and four $15 T-shirts. _____

7. Esteban bought a $35 pair of pants and two $20 T-shirts. _____

8. Diana bought two $18 skirts and a $5 pair of earrings. _____

Dog Walk

Scooter starts his walk at home. Then, he walks from each point to the next, as listed below. Mark each stop with a point and its letter. Connect the stops in order to draw Scooter's complete path. Round to the nearest whole number.

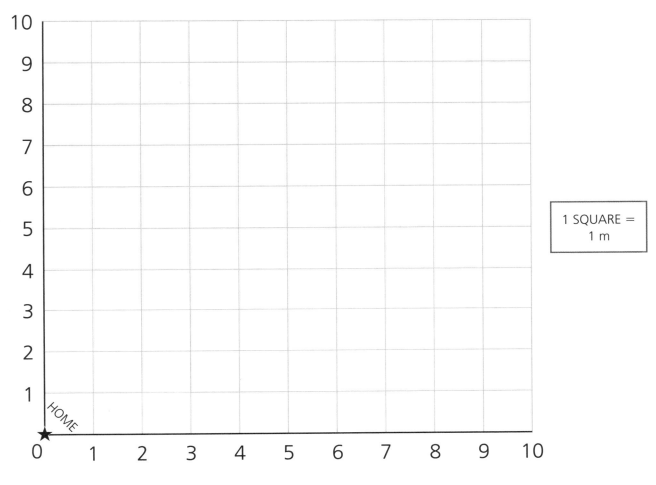

1 SQUARE = 1 m

A. $\frac{51}{17}$ m north _____

B. 600 cm east _____

C. 0.002 km south _____

D. 4,000 mm west _____

E. $\sqrt{36}$ m north _____

F. 2π m east _____

G. $\frac{86}{43}$ m south _____

H. $3(10^2)$ cm west _____

I. 4(0.001) km north _____

J. $5(10^3)$ mm east _____

1. How many total meters did Scooter walk to get to point J? _____

2. How many total feet did Scooter walk to get to point J and then back home again? Assume he followed the same path both ways. Round to the nearest whole number. _____

Fun in the Sun

Solve each equation for the missing variable. Then take the variable letter and place it on the line below that corresponds with the correct answer. You will spell out the title to a classic summer tune.

1. $\dfrac{5}{3} = \dfrac{40}{u}$ _____

2. $162{:}61.2 = 270{:}n$ _____

3. $\dfrac{i}{13} = \dfrac{90}{117}$ _____

4. $\dfrac{51}{17} = \dfrac{9}{f}$ _____

5. $65{:}s = 35{:}168$ _____

6. $\dfrac{1.42}{71} = \dfrac{a}{213}$ _____

7. $r{:}30 = 30{:}120$ _____

8. $\dfrac{28}{i} = \dfrac{44}{858}$ _____

9. $\dfrac{63}{9} = \dfrac{7}{f}$ _____

10. $91{:}13 = a{:}1$ _____

11. $144{:}1.44 = 20{:}s$ _____

12. $\dfrac{144}{r} = \dfrac{36}{.3}$ _____

____ ____ ____ ____ ____ ____   ____ ____ ____ ____ ____ ____
0.2   24   7.5   1   546   102   312   7   3   4.26   1.2   10

Late at the Library

Use the information in the box to answer the questions below.

> **Lexington Public Library Late Fees**
>
> Books: 5 cents per day
>
> Audiobooks: 15 cents per day
>
> DVDs: $2 per day

1. Gus has the following items checked out from the Lexington Public Library: 6 books, 3 DVDs, and 1 audiobook. The books and audiobook are 13 days overdue. The DVDs are 3 days overdue. How much money does Gus owe the library in late fees? _____

2. Dorian has 2 DVDs that are 2 days overdue and her sister Kat has 33 books that are 7 days overdue. How much money do they owe the library in late fees? _____

3. Gina has 9 audiobooks that are 2 weeks overdue and 5 books that are 1 day overdue. How much money does she owe the library in late fees? _____

4. Quincy has 8 books that were due 2 days ago and 17 books due tomorrow. How much money does he owe the library in late fees? _____

5. Courtney has twice as many books as DVDs. They are all 3 days late. Courtney owes less than $26, but more than $25. How many books does she have checked out from the library? _____

6. Alicia owes $5.80. Her items are 2 days overdue. She has only one type of item checked out. What is she returning to the library? _____

7. Vinny lost his library book and must pay to replace it. He owes 6.2 times the amount that Alicia owed after 1 day. How much money does Vinny owe the library? _____

8. The Lexington Public Library is open for the same number of hours every Monday, Tuesday, Wednesday, and Friday. It stays open 2 hours longer on Thursday than it does on Monday, Tuesday, Wednesday, or Friday. It is open for 4 hours on Saturday and is closed on Sundays. If the library is open 2,760 minutes per week, how many hours is it open on Tuesdays? _____

Chart It!

Choose the type of graph or diagram that would best fit each situation.

1. Eric wants to show how he spends the money he makes from raking leaves.

    a. line graph
    b. pie chart
    c. scatter plot
    d. bar graph

2. Monica wants to show on the same graph the average monthly rainfall and the average monthly temperature of her hometown.

    a. line graph
    b. pie chart
    c. bar graph
    d. both a and c

3. Amrit wants to show how many of his classmates take French, how many take German, and how many take both.

    a. scatter plot
    b. Venn diagram
    c. bar graph
    d. pie chart

4. Hayley wants to show the frequency of height in inches of the people in her class.

    a. histogram
    b. Venn diagram
    c. pie chart
    d. table

5. Luke wants to represent his weight loss over 12 weeks.

    a. pie chart
    b. line graph
    c. histogram
    d. Venn diagram

6. Zahara wants to show the percentages of people who order different flavors of soda in the cafeteria.

    a. histogram
    b. scatter plot
    c. Venn diagram
    d. pie chart

7. Dwight wants to show the relationship between vehicle speed and traffic accidents.

    a. Venn diagram
    b. scatter plot
    c. bar graph
    d. pie chart

8. Mark wants to show the statistics for his soccer team.

    a. Venn diagram
    b. scatter plot
    c. table
    d. pie chart

Before the Flood

Use the information in the box to solve the problems below.

Jacob lives on a farm, and the nearby river is due to flood his farm after the upcoming storm. Jacob needs to transport his animals and food across the river before the flood. Jacob has a small rowboat that has only enough space for Jacob and either his dingo, his bunny, or his basket of carrots. Jacob has a problem. If he leaves the bunny alone with the carrots, the bunny will eat the carrots. If Jacob leaves the bunny alone with the dingo, the dingo will eat the bunny.

1. How can Jacob get his dingo, his bunny, and his carrots across the river?

_____

_____

_____

_____

_____

_____

_____

2. How many one-way trips will Jacob have to make to accomplish this?

_____

45

We All Scream for Ice Cream!

On the school trip, everyone gets an ice cream treat. Use the information on the menu to answer the questions below.

1. How many different treats are available if each student can choose one ice cream flavor, one topping, and one cone? _____

2. There are 30 students on the class trip. If 20% of the students are having strawberry ice cream, how many students will be having either chocolate or vanilla? _____

3. If each ice cream treat cost $2.35, how much did all the treats cost together? _____

4. The ratio of those who ordered cake cones to waffle cones is 2:3. How many students ordered waffle cones? _____

5. In a poll of 1,200 students, 600 said they preferred vanilla ice cream, 400 chose chocolate ice cream, and 200 students chose strawberry. How many students in this class are likely to order chocolate ice cream? _____

6. Based on the poll, what proportion of the class will order vanilla or strawberry ice cream? _____

7. The snack bar runs out of strawberry ice cream. How many different types of ice cream treat options are there to choose from now? _____

A Tale of Two Angles

Give the complementary angle to each angle listed.

1. 57° _____

2. 28° _____

3. 89° _____

4. 17° _____

5. 63° _____

6. 45° _____

Now give the supplementary angle to each angle listed.

7. 110° _____

8. 36° _____

9. 65° _____

10. 90° _____

11. 170° _____

12. 125° _____

The Calculating Cook

Read each complete recipe. Then fill in each duplicate recipe that follows with the equivalent measurements that are requested.

Applesauce

4 cups apples, peeled, cored, and cut into thick slices

3 tablespoons water

$\frac{1}{2}$ cup brown sugar

$\frac{1}{4}$ cup lemon juice

$\frac{1}{4}$ teaspoon nutmeg

1 teaspoon ($\frac{1}{3}$ tablespoon) cinnamon

2 tablespoons ($\frac{1}{8}$ cup) butter

Place the peeled, cored, and diced apples in a saucepan. Add water, brown sugar, lemon juice, nutmeg, and cinnamon. Cover and cook over medium-low heat until apples are tender. This takes 20–30 minutes. Remove cover and cook for an additional 5 minutes to allow some of the moisture to evaporate. Stir in butter. Serve warm or cold.

Applesauce

_____ pints apples, peeled, cored and cut into thick slices

_____ cups water

_____ pints brown sugar

_____ tablespoons lemon juice

_____ tablespoon nutmeg

1 teaspoon ($\frac{1}{3}$ tablespoon) cinnamon

_____ teaspoons butter

Place the peeled, cored, and diced apples in a saucepan. Add water, brown sugar, lemon juice, nutmeg, and cinnamon. Cover and cook over medium-low heat until apples are tender. This takes _____ hours. Remove cover and cook for an additional _____ seconds to allow some of the moisture to evaporate. Stir in butter. Serve warm or cold.

Porcupine Meatballs

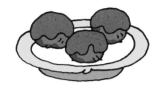

$\frac{1}{2}$ pound ground beef

$\frac{1}{2}$ pound ground pork

$\frac{1}{4}$ cup rice

1 cup onion, chopped

3 tablespoons butter

3 8-ounce cans tomato sauce

$\frac{2}{3}$ cup water

$\frac{1}{2}$ teaspoon parsley flakes

1 ounce bacon, cut into small pieces

Salt and pepper to taste

Preheat oven to 325°F. Mix beef and pork together. Add salt, pepper, and rice. Sauté onion in butter. Cool. Add to meat mixture. Form into meatballs. Mix tomato sauce and water in a bowl. Pour over meatballs. Sprinkle with parsley flakes. Top with bacon pieces. Cook covered for 75 minutes at 325°F. Let stand 15 minutes before serving.

Porcupine Meatballs

_____ ounces ground beef

$\frac{1}{2}$ pound ground pork

_____ teaspoons rice

_____ pint onion, chopped

3 tablespoons butter

3 _____-cup cans tomato sauce

_____ quart water

$\frac{1}{2}$ teaspoon parsley flakes

_____ pound bacon, cut into small pieces

Salt and pepper to taste

Preheat oven to _____°C. Mix beef and pork together. Add salt, pepper, and rice. Sauté onion in butter. Cool. Add to meat mixture. Form into meatballs. Mix tomato sauce and water in a bowl. Pour over meatballs. Sprinkle with parsley flakes. Top with bacon pieces. Cook covered for _____ hours at 325°F. Let stand 15 minutes before serving.

Hockey Gear

Use the information provided to solve the problems below.

Micah, Zoey, and Avery shopped for hockey gear at their local ice rink's going-out-of-business sale. Avery bought two items and received $3.50 in change from a $50 bill. Avery and Zoey each purchased one item that was the same as the other's. Micah spent $0.50 less on the one item he purchased than Zoey spent on the two items she purchased.

1. What did each person buy?

_____

_____

_____

2. How much did each person spend?

_____

_____

_____

Messy Metrics

Use your knowledge of metrics to match each measurement in Column A to a measurement of equal value in Column B. Round up or down if needed.

Column A	Column B
1. 0.7 gram	**A.** 0.01 ounce
2. 7 grams	**B.** 15 kilograms
3. 3 kilograms	**C.** 7,000 milligrams
4. 3,000 kilograms	**D.** 15,000 kilograms
5. 15 metric tons	**E.** 100,000 grams
6. 70 grams	**F.** 330 grams
7. 15,000 grams	**G.** 2.47 ounces
8. 0.33 kilogram	**H.** 3 metric tons
9. 0.33 gram	**I.** 700 milligrams
10. $\frac{3}{4}$ metric ton	**J.** 1,000,000 milligrams
11. 1 kilogram	**K.** 750 kilograms
12. 100 kilograms	**L.** 6.6 pounds

Big Foot

Did you know that you can estimate the surface area of your body using your foot?
It's simple. Just perform the steps that follow, and use the example to guide you. Write your measurements.

1. Place one of your bare feet on the graph paper on the next page.

2. Use a pencil to trace the outline of your foot onto the graph paper. Example:

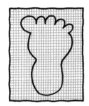

3. Remove your foot. Now, count the whole number of centimeter squares your foot fills. Write the answer below. Example:

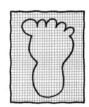 336 whole squares

4. Next, count the number of partial centimeter squares your foot fills. Write the answer below. Example:

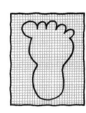 50 partial squares

5. Add these two numbers to get a whole number estimate of the area of your foot. Write the answer below. Example:

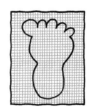 336 + 50 = 386

6. To determine the surface area of your entire body, multiply your foot's area by 100. Write the answer below. Example:

 386 × 100 = 38,600 square centimeters

MY MEASUREMENTS

Whole number of centimeter squares my foot fills: _____

Partial centimeter squares my foot fills: _____

My footprint is about _____ square centimeters.

The surface area of my body is about _____ square centimeters.

Money Matters

American paper bills all weigh about 0.03 ounce and are about 2.5 inches wide, 6 inches long, and 0.0004 inch thick. Use this information to answer the questions below.

1. The dimensions of a table are 9 feet by 5 feet. How many bills would be needed to cover it completely? _____

2. The circumference of earth is about 25,000 miles. How many bills laid end to end would it take to equal that? _____

3. The Sears Tower is 1,454 feet high. If you laid $5 bills end to end to match that height, how much money would you have? _____

4. A container of milk weighs 32 ounces. How many bills equal this weight? _____

5. An ostrich weighs 345 pounds. If you had a stack of $20 bills equal to that weight, how much money would you have? _____

6. How many bills would it take, lined up end to end, to equal your height? _____

7. How many bills would it take to equal your weight? _____

8. What is the "value" of your weight in $10 bills? _____

Birthday Boxes

Isabel has already received eight gifts for her 12th birthday tomorrow. She is trying to guess what might fit inside each gift box. Help Isabel by finding the volume of each box. Express your answer in cubic inches. Round your answer to the nearest tenth.

1.

l = 24 in   w = 18 in   h = 12 in
_____

2.
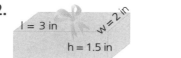
l = 3 in   w = 2 in   h = 1.5 in
_____

3.

l = 9 in   w = 9 in   h = 9 in
_____

4.

l = 5 in   w = 3 in   h = 3 in
_____

5.

l = 10 in   w = 5 in   h = 20 in
_____

6.

l = 10.16 cm   w = 12.7 cm   h = 20.32 cm
_____

7.

l = 2 in   w = 2 in   h = 1 in
_____

8.

l = 16 in   w = 16 in   h = 30 in
_____

9. Isabel received a tiny pair of diamond stud earrings for her birthday. Which box were they likely in? _____

10. Isabel received a 27-inch flat screen television for her birthday. Which box was it likely in? _____

Popular Vote

In the town of Charlottesville, 34,000 residents cast a vote in the latest mayoral election.
This pie graph shows how they voted. Use it to complete the table, then answer the questions below.

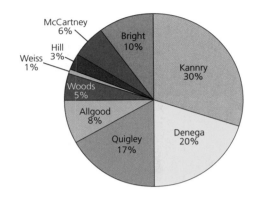

Candidate	Percent of Votes as a Decimal	Number of Votes
Kannry		
Denega		
Quigley		
Allgood		
Woods		
Weiss		
Hill		
McCartney		
Bright		
Total		

1. Who won the mayoral election? _____

2. What margin separates the winner from the person who came in second? Express your answer as
   a whole number. _____

3. What is the mean number of votes received by the candidates? Round your answer to the nearest
   whole number. _____

4. How does candidate Weiss affect the mean? Explain. _____

_____

Hot Tips

Part of Joe's salary as a taxi driver comes from tips that people give him. Calculate the tips for each of the amounts below.

1. 15% of $22.10   _____

2. 18% of $47.54   _____

3. 17.5% of $12.13   _____

4. 15% of $119.87   _____

5. 19% of $29.98   _____

6. 20% of $15.72   _____

7. 16% of $58. 01   _____

8. 20% of $40.40   _____

Use rounding and estimating to determine the tips below.

9. 15% of $49.57   _____

10. 20% of $40.53   _____

Using the information provided, answer the questions below.

11. Denise left a 20% tip for a taxi driver. The tip was $7.28. How much was the ride? _____

12. Gerard left a 15% tip for a taxi driver. The tip was $1.41. How much was the ride? _____

Next Stop: Nevada!

Nevada is one of the fastest growing states in America. Use the chart to answer the questions below.

POPULATION OF NEVADA: 2000–2007

Year	Population
2000	2,018,494
2001	2,095,331
2002	2,167,645
2003	2,238,336
2004	2,329,960
2005	2,408,948
2006	2,492,427
2007	2,565,382

1. How many more people lived in Nevada in 2005 than in 2001? _____

2. How many more people lived in Nevada in 2007 than in 2004? _____

3. How many more people lived in Nevada in 2007 than in 2000? _____

4. What was the population growth percentage from 2000 to 2007? _____

5. If the population grows 10% from 2007 to 2010, what will the population of Nevada be in 2010? _____

6. Draw a line graph based on the chart above. Use your graph to answer questions 7 and 8.

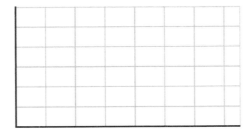

7. Between which years was growth the greatest? _____

8. Between which years was growth the smallest? _____

It's a Draw!

Draw a picture of each of the triangles described below. Then answer the questions.

1. Draw a scalene triangle.

2. Draw a right isosceles triangle.

3. Draw an equilateral triangle.

4. Draw an obtuse triangle.

5. Draw an acute triangle.

6. Draw an isosceles triangle with no right angles.

7. Can an acute triangle contain a right angle?

_____

8. If a right triangle has a 37° angle, what are the other two angles?

_____   _____

Party Time!

Use the following recipe to answer the questions below.

Snack Mix

Serves 12

$2\frac{1}{2}$ cups pretzels $3\frac{3}{4}$ cups potato chips

$1\frac{1}{4}$ cups peanuts $2\frac{2}{3}$ cups cheese puffs

$3\frac{1}{3}$ cups corn chips $1\frac{2}{3}$ cups almonds

1. What is the total number of cups of ingredients used to make the recipe? _____

2. If Molly eats $1\frac{1}{2}$ cups, Jake eats $\frac{3}{4}$ cup, and Ali eats $2\frac{2}{3}$ cups, how much snack mix will be left?

_____

3. For one recipe, pretzels cost $.96, peanuts cost $2.29, corn chips cost $1.35, potato chips cost $.89, cheese puffs cost $1.98, and almonds cost $2.39. You purchase enough ingredients for 1 complete recipe. How much change will you receive if you pay with a 10-dollar bill? _____

4. Your guests really love chips! If you doubled the potato chips and tripled the corn chips, how many total cups of snack mix would there be? _____

5. You need to make enough mix for 30 people. Cheese puffs are sold in $1\frac{1}{2}$-cup bags. How many bags of cheese puffs will you need to buy? _____

6. Two of your friends are allergic to nuts, so you leave the nuts out of the recipe. How many cups of snack mix would one recipe make now? _____

7. It takes your guests 90 minutes to eat one batch of snack mix. If you want to make enough mix to last for three hours, how many cups of potato chips will you need to buy? _____

8. Using the information you learned in question #7, determine how much snack mix your guests will eat in one hour. Give your answer in cups. _____

Recipe Reminders

Use the information provided to answer the questions below.

Abby's grandmother sent her a copy of her recipes. Grandma uses some unusual measurements, so Abby made note cards to help her remember the measurements in her favorite recipes.

1. When Abby's recipes didn't turn out as planned, she asked her mother to check her note cards to see if she had made any mistakes. Abby's mother said that 3 of the note cards are incorrect. Which ones are incorrect?

_____

_____

_____

2. Now, rewrite the incorrect cards to make them right. Write the correct measurement equivalents on the lines below.

_____

_____

_____

Sail Away!

Use the diagrams to answer the questions below.

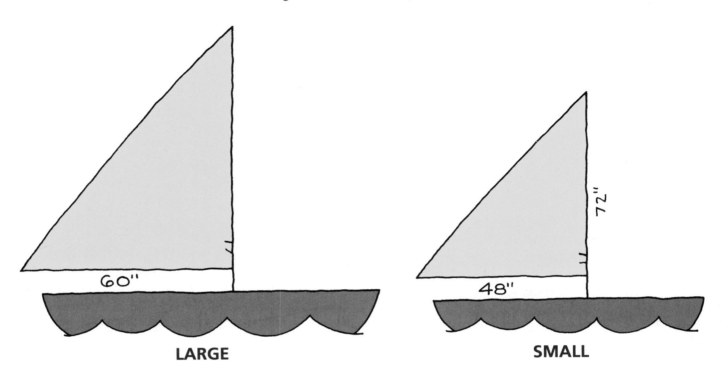

LARGE

SMALL

1. The Salty Sea Dog Sailboat Company makes sails in two sizes: small and large. The sails are in proportion to each other. How tall is the large sail? _____

2. The company needs to make two small sails. How much material does it need? Give your answer in square feet. _____

3. The company has an order for 3 large sails and 1 small sail. How much material does it need? Give your answer in square feet. _____

4. The company is introducing an extra-large sail that is in proportion to the other two sails. If the length of the sail is 84 inches, how tall is the sail? _____

5. What is the area of the extra-large sail in square feet? _____

Largest of Them All

Write the largest number that meets each set of criteria.

1. There are 10 total digits. There is a 5 in the billions place. __5,999,999,999__

2. Each digit from 1 through 7 (including 1 and 7) is used one time each. There is a 2 in the ten thousands place. __7,625,431__

3. Each digit from 5 through 9 (including 5 and 9) is used one time each. There is a 5 in the thousands place. __95,876__

4. The digit in the hundred billions place is one less than the digit in the hundred millions place. The digit in the hundred millions place is one less than the digit in the hundred thousands place. There are 12 total digits in the number. __799,899,999,999__

5. Each digit from 2 through 6 (including 2 and 6) is used one time each. There is a 4 in the ones place. __65,324__

6. Each digit from 3 through 8 (including 3 and 8) is used one time each. There is a 6 in the tens place. There is a 4 in the hundred thousands place. __487,563__

Ice Caper

Use the information provided to answer the questions below.

RINK A   RINK B

100 ft

1. Flo Frost performs triple jumps on Rink A. When she reaches the edge of the ice, she realizes that her hat has fallen off at the center of the rink. She has to skate 40 feet in order to go back and get it. What is the radius of the ice rink? _____

2. Using the information in question 1, determine the circumference of the ice rink.

_____

3. After Flo picks up her hat, a Zamboni machine arrives to resurface the ice. What is the area of the ice that the driver must cover? _____

4. Flo is competing at an event on Rink B. What is the area of that rink? _____

5. How much larger is the area of Rink B than Rink A? _____

Fraction Action

Answer the questions below.

1. Which is the largest fraction: $\frac{1}{6}$, $\frac{1}{8}$, $\frac{3}{16}$? _____

2. Which is the smallest fraction: $-\frac{1}{4}$, $-\frac{2}{5}$, $-\frac{3}{7}$? _____

3. $\frac{2}{9^3} - \frac{1}{9} =$ _____

4. $\frac{2}{3} \times \frac{1}{4} \times \frac{6}{16} =$ _____

5. What is the average of the following fractions: $\frac{1}{4}$, $\frac{2}{3}$, $\frac{1}{8}$? _____

6. A rectangle has a length of $\frac{3}{4}$ inch and a width of $\frac{1}{2}$ inch. What is the perimeter?

_____

7. What is the area of the rectangle in question 6? _____

8. What is $\frac{1}{5}$ of a year? _____

9. The student council needs a $\frac{2}{3}$ majority for a motion to pass. There are 81 members. What is the minimum number of student council members who have to vote "yes" for a motion to pass? _____

10. What does $\frac{2}{3}$ of a 12-ounce bag of pretzels weigh? _____

Are We There Yet?

Answer the questions below.

1. It takes Dana and her mother 30 minutes to travel 20 miles. How long will it take them to travel 35 miles moving at the same rate? _____

2. It took Macklin 2 hours to travel 80 miles to the theme park. How long will it take him to return home if he travels 10 miles per hour faster on the return trip? _____

3. Rafael runs 5 miles in 45 minutes. At this rate, how long will it take him to run 8 miles?

_____

4. Ashleigh biked 3 miles in 12 minutes. At this rate, how far can she travel in 30 minutes?

_____

5. Cecilia's train traveled 240 miles in 3 hours. How far will it travel in 5.5 hours? _____

6. Luke's train traveled at 270 km/hr for 2 hours, 12 minutes. How far did the train travel?

_____

7. Car A traveled 110 miles in 2.2 hours. Car B traveled 280 miles in 5.1 hours. Which car traveled faster? _____

8. Angel ran 9 miles in 58 minutes. Derek ran 11 miles in 67 minutes. Who ran faster? _____

Market Measure

Search your school and home for boxes of each of the items listed below. Use them to answer the questions that follow.

1. Measure each box. Record its measurements, then determine its volume.

Box	Width	Height	Length	Volume
Raisins				
Cereal				
Crackers				
Toothpicks				
Rice				
Pasta				

2. Which box has the smallest volume? _____

3. Which box has the largest volume? _____

4. What is the difference between the smallest and largest volumes? _____

5. How many of the smallest boxes would fit inside the largest box? _____

6. Determine the mean width of your boxes. _____

7. Determine the median height of your boxes. _____

8. Is there a mode for width, height, length, or volume of your boxes? If so, write it here.

_____

Pizza Puzzler

Use the menu and the information provided to answer the questions below.

Max, Allie, Arden, Oliver, and Lily met for dinner at Pasquale's Pizzeria. They ordered a large mushroom pizza, a small pepperoni and pineapple pizza, and four bottles of water.

Pasquale's Pizzeria Menu

Large Pizza (8 Slices) $14⁰⁰
Small Pizza (6 Slices) $11⁵⁰
Soda $1⁷⁵
Bottled Water $2⁰⁰

Toppings $1⁵⁰ Each
Choices: Pepperoni, Meatballs, Mushrooms, Onions, Green Peppers, Anchovies, Pineapple

Tax Included in Prices
15% tip will be added for parties of 5 or more.

1. Oliver ate twice as many slices as Max. Allie, Arden, and Lily ate two slices each. There were two slices left over. How many slices did Max eat? _____

2. Who ate more slices: Arden or Max? _____

3. What percentage of the pizza slices did Oliver eat? Round your answer to the nearest whole number. _____

4. The friends shared the bill equally. How much did each person owe? _____

5. Allie's mom bought a large pizza with mushrooms, onions, and peppers. How much did it cost per slice? _____

6. Which is cheaper: 10 small cheese pizzas or 6 large meatball pizzas? _____

7. If you want two toppings on your pizza, how many different pizza topping combinations could you order at Pasquale's Pizzeria? _____

8. Your aunt is a vegetarian who eats only vegetables, fruits, and fish. If she wanted two toppings on her pizza, how many combinations could she order at Pasquale's? _____

Buyer Beware

Margarita is shopping for a new car while interest rates at the dealer are at 0%.
There are many different models from which to choose. Fill in the missing information in each scenario.

1. Model: Ural GT. A compact hatchback.

Fuel: 29 mpg highway

Price: $13,000

Down payment: $1,000

Term: 24 months

Monthly payment: _____

2. Model: Carbly SX. A four-door sedan.

Fuel: 26 mpg highway

Price: $17,500

Down payment: _____

Term: 36 months

Monthly payment: $416.67

3. Model: QD Cruiser. A small SUV.

Fuel: 24 mpg highway

Price: $15,000

Down payment: $3,000

Term: _____ months

Monthly payment: $166.67

4. Model: QD Cruiser Sport. A faster, sportier version of the QD Cruiser.

Fuel: 21 mpg highway

Price: _____

Down payment: $4,500

Term: 60 months

Monthly payment: $200.00

5. Model: Prium. A compact, hatchback hybrid.

Fuel: 33 mpg highway

Price: $21,500

Down payment: $750

Term: 48 months

Monthly payment: _____

6. Model: Mountaineer. A large, luxury SUV.

Fuel: 18 mpg highway

Price: $27,000

Down payment: _____

Term: 36 months

Monthly payment: $611.11

7. Model: Mica TS. A small four-door sedan.

Fuel: 28 mpg highway

Price: _____

Down payment: $3,300

Term: 60 months

Monthly payment: $261.67

8. Model: Mica Hybrid. A small four-door sedan with hybrid technology.

Fuel: 31 mpg highway

Price: $22,500

Down payment: $4,500

Term: 48 months

Monthly payment: _____

9. If you had to pick one of these cars to purchase, which one would it be? Explain. _____

_____

Angle Puzzle

Use the diagram to determine the measure of the angles below.

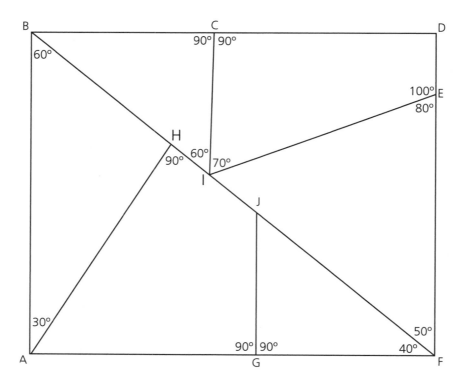

1. ∠ CDE _____

2. ∠ GJF _____

3. ∠ HJG _____

4. ∠ CBI _____

5. ∠ AHB _____

6. ∠ EIF _____

Poison Ivy

Help Mila avoid the poison ivy in her backyard! Indicate whether there is a poison ivy leaf at each set of coordinates by writing *yes* or *no*.

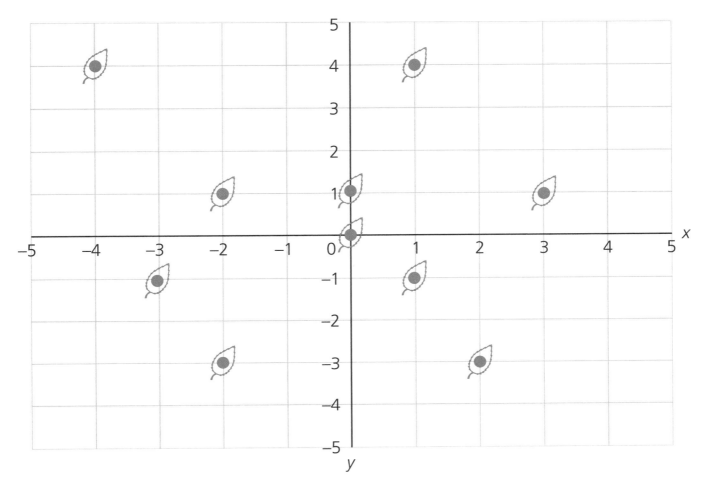

1. (3, 1) _____

2. (–4, 4) _____

3. (5, 1) _____

4. (1, –1) _____

5. (1, 4) _____

6. (0, –3) _____

7. (–1, 1) _____

8. (0, 0) _____

Remote Control Ratios

Use the information provided to answer the questions below. Express your answers in lowest terms.

1. Rachel's television carries channels 01 to 99. How many channels begin with 2? Express your answer as a ratio in lowest terms. _____

2. How many of Rachel's channels have an 8 in them? Express your answer as a ratio in lowest terms. _____

3. Rachel's favorite show airs on channel 33 four times a day. The show lasts for half an hour. How much of channel 33's daily programming does that represent? Express your answer as a ratio in lowest terms. _____

4. A program that lasts one hour has 14 minutes of commercials. What is the ratio of commercials to television show in lowest terms? _____

5. The public television station carries 4 hours of children's programming per day. The remaining shows are adult educational programming. What is the ratio of children's programming to adult educational programming in lowest terms? _____

6. Ted Mogul owns several television stations in Badgerville. The ratio of stations that he owns to the total number of stations in Badgerville is 1:25. If there are 225 stations, how many stations does he own? _____

7. This week, *Pop Star Pick* had 31.7 million viewers. Last week, it had 5% fewer viewers. What is the ratio of last week's viewership to this week's in lowest terms? _____

8. Rachel's parents allow her to watch 2 hours of television per day. What is the ratio of her weekly television viewing hours to the total number of hours per week in lowest terms? _____

9. Collin's television carries channels 2 to 345. How many channels begin with 4? _____

10. Edward's parents allow him to watch 3 hours of television per day, every day of the week. He also spends 3 hours a day doing homework on weekdays. What is the ratio of his weekly television viewing hours to weekly homework hours in lowest terms? _____

11. This week, *Dancing with a Celebrity* had 34.5 million viewers. Last week, it had 2% more viewers. What is the ratio of last week's viewership to this week's in lowest terms? _____

12. A program that lasts 30 minutes has 11 minutes of commercials. What is the ratio of commercials to television show in lowest terms? _____

How Many Miles in the Nile?

The chart below lists some of the world's longest rivers. Use it to answer the questions below.

Name	Length (miles)	Location
Nile	4,160	Africa
Amazon	4,000	South America
Yangtze	3,900	China
Huang He	3,000	China
Ob	2,268	Russia
Amur	2,744	Asia
Lena	2,734	Russia
Congo	2,900	Africa
Paraná	2,485	South America
Mekong	2,600	Asia

1. What percentage of the rivers is in Africa? _____

2. What percentage of the rivers is not in Europe or Asia? _____

3. The Mississippi is the longest river in the United States. It is 2,340 miles long. How much longer is the Nile than the Mississippi? Express your answer as a percentage. Round to the nearest whole number. _____

4. What is the mean length of the 3 longest rivers? Round to the nearest whole number.

_____

5. What is the range of the 3 longest rivers? _____

6. Convert your answer to the previous question into feet. _____

7. What is the median of the rivers shown in the chart? _____

8. What is the mean length of the rivers? Round to the nearest whole number.

_____

The Lineup

Express the following fractions as decimals. Round your answer to the nearest hundredth and write the number on the line. Then place each answer on the number line.

1. $-\frac{3}{5}$ _____

2. $\frac{2}{3}$ _____

3. $\frac{5}{9}$ _____

4. $\frac{13}{7}$ _____

5. $-\frac{5}{4}$ _____

6. $\frac{11}{8}$ _____

7. $-\frac{1}{6}$ _____

8. $-\frac{2}{7}$ _____

9. $\frac{67}{81}$ _____

10. $\frac{3}{19}$ _____

11. $\frac{1}{99}$ _____

12. $\frac{10}{21}$ _____

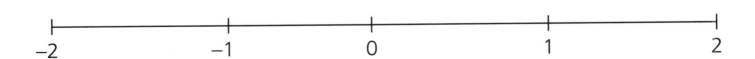

$-2 \qquad -1 \qquad 0 \qquad 1 \qquad 2$

Say Ahh!

Nurse Mabel is performing her daily rounds. Use the information provided to answer the questions below.

1. Bob needs a new Band-Aid. Mabel applies a fresh Band-Aid and looks at the box. Just 7 Band-Aids remain in a box of 350. What percentage of the Band-Aids have been used? _____

2. Ada needs liquid vitamins. Nurse Mabel administers 7.5 milliliters to her per day. How many teaspoons is that? (Hint: 5 milliliters = 1 teaspoon.) _____

3. Nurse Mabel gives Violet a $\frac{1}{2}$ teaspoon of medication every 4 hours. How many milliliters does she get per day? _____

4. How many teaspoons are there in 1 liter? _____

5. Jerry has been in the hospital for 4 days. It's April. What percentage of the month has he been in the hospital? Round your answer to the nearest whole number. _____

6. Nurse Mabel checks Anita's blood pressure. It is 125 over 80 ($\frac{125}{80}$). Yesterday, the systolic pressure (the top number) was 4% lower. Her diastolic pressure (bottom number) was the same as today. What was her blood pressure yesterday? _____

7. Reena fell and broke 4 bones. Humans have 206 bones in their bodies. What percentage of her bones did Reena break? _____

8. Nurse Mabel works an 8-hour shift. She has worked 37.5% of her shift. How much time does she have left?_____

Good Sport

Use proportions to solve the following problems.

1. While jumping hurdles, members of the track team usually bang their knees about 35 times in 4 hours of practice. How many knee bangs would they experience in 30 hours of practice? _____

2. Marathon Man lost 45 minutes over 3 races due to a sprained ankle. At this rate, how much time will be lost in 7 races? _____

3. The school newspaper asked 20 soccer players if they felt the program should buy new uniforms. Of those asked, 12 said yes. At that rate, if there are 80 students in the school soccer program, how many will want new uniforms? _____

4. Out of every 9 joggers who suffer heel spurs, 7 are men. Out of 504 heel spurs, how many sufferers are men? _____

5. Last year, 350 out of 500 hockey injuries were injuries to the neck. Of each of the 10 hockey injuries, how many are to the neck? _____

6. The ratio of strikes to swings for Baseball Barry is 4 strikes to every 15 swings. At this rate, how many times will Barry **not** get a strike if he takes 360 swings? _____

7. The cost of hospital visits for Boxer Bob averages $900.00 for two months of competition. At this rate, how much will hospital visits cost in a 5-month-long competitive season? _____

8. Out of every 7 members of the volleyball team, 2 have to drop out before the end of the season due to wrist injury. If 28 drop out because of wrist injury, how many started the season? _____

Out of This World

Use the information provided to answer the questions below.

1. Jupiter's radius is about 43,411 miles. What is its diameter? _____

2. Earth's radius is 3,959 miles. What is its diameter? _____

3. Mercury has a diameter of 3,032 miles. What is its radius? _____

4. Ganymede, Jupiter's largest moon, has a radius of 1,635 miles. Earth's moon has a radius of 1,080 miles. How much larger is Ganymede's circumference than the moon's circumference?

_____

5. Mars has a radius that is 41,305 miles smaller than Jupiter's radius. What is the radius of Mars?

_____

6. Wind speed on Saturn can reach 1,800 kilometers per hour. Give this measurement in miles per hour (hint: 1 kilometer = 0.62137 miles). Round your answer to the nearest whole number.

_____

7. Earth's average surface temperature is 14°C. Give this temperature in degrees Fahrenheit. Round your answer to the nearest whole number. _____

8. True or false: Saturn's radius > 43,411 miles? _____

A Day at the Farm

Farmer Brown is getting ready to plant his crops. Use the diagram of the field to answer the questions below.

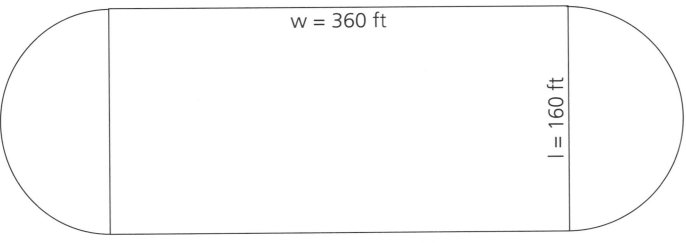

w = 360 ft

l = 160 ft

Farmer Brown's Field

1. What is the area of Farmer Brown's field? _____

2. Farmer Brown wants to plant corn on 45% of his field. How many square feet of land will be used for corn? Round your answer to the nearest whole number. _____

3. Farmer Brown will grow summer squash on $\frac{1}{8}$ of his field. How many square feet of land will be used for summer squash? _____

4. If Farmer Brown plants $\frac{2}{5}$ of the field with soybeans, $\frac{1}{10}$ with cucumbers, and $\frac{1}{2}$ with corn, how many square feet of the field are left over? _____

5. Farmer Brown has planted sunflowers, pumpkins, and radishes. He used 25% of the field for radishes. There is twice as much land being used for pumpkins as there is for sunflowers. How many square feet of the field are used for pumpkins? _____

6. Farmer Brown has decided not to plant crops in the circular areas of his field this year. How many square feet of the field will be planted? _____

Common Language

The most commonly used words in the English language are listed in order of frequency in the chart below. Choose a paragraph or passage with 100 words from your favorite book. Each time you find one of the words on the chart, add a mark to the tally. Then record the total number of times each word appears in the passage.

YOUR FAVORITE CHAPTER BOOK

Word	Tally	Total
THE		
OF		
AND		
TO		
A		
IN		
THAT		
IS		
I		
IT		
FOR		
AS		

1. According to your findings, rank the words in descending order of appearance.

_____   _____

_____   _____

_____   _____

_____   _____

_____   _____

_____   _____

2. How does the frequency of the words in your book compare to the order of the words in the language as a whole? _____

_____

3. Which word occurred most often in your tally? _____

Now, choose a paragraph or passage with 100 words from your math textbook.
As before, each time you find one of the words on the chart, add a mark to the tally.
Then record the total number of times each word appears in the passage.

YOUR MATH TEXTBOOK

Word	Tally	Total
THE		
OF		
AND		
TO		
A		
IN		
THAT		
IS		
I		
IT		
FOR		
AS		

4. According to your findings, rank the words in descending order of appearance.

_____   _____

_____   _____

_____   _____

_____   _____

_____   _____

_____   _____

5. How does the frequency of the words in your math textbook compare to the order of the words in your favorite book? Explain. _____

_____

6. Based on this tally, what is the probability of the word *and* appearing in any random passage of 100 words? _____

Yum Yum in the Tum Tum

Use the information on the menu to answer the following questions about the Yum Yum Fudge Hut.

Jackie buys a pound each of Milk Chocolate, Nutty Fudge, and Pistachio. She negotiates a deal in which she gets the lowest price pound of candy for $\frac{1}{2}$ off.

Wyatt gets .25 lb of each kind. Olivia buys $\frac{1}{3}$ pound of Butterscotch, $\frac{1}{2}$ lb of Peanut Butter, and 0.75 lb of Praline Pecan. Allegra spends .45 of what Jackie spends plus $\frac{4}{5}$ of what Wyatt spends. How much did each of them spend?

1. Jackie _____

2. Wyatt _____

3. Olivia _____

4. Allegra _____

5. Olivia realizes she also wanted to get some Mint Chip. If she has $1.85 left, does she have enough money? _____

6. At Yum Yum's summer opening celebration, 50 people were offered free fudge. They had 2 choices of flavors: Milk Chocolate or Nutty Fudge. Some people took 1 of each kind. If 20 people took Milk Chocolate and 17 people also took Milk Chocolate and Nutty Fudge, how many people took only Nutty Fudge? _____

7. Neil has a nut allergy. If he picks one of the fudges offered at the Yum Yum Fudge Hut at random, what is the likelihood that he will *not* be able to eat it? Express as a fraction. _____

8. Macy has exactly $16.75 to spend at the Yum Yum Fudge Hut. She wants to get equal amounts of each type of fudge offered. How much of each type of fudge can she purchase if tax is 5%?

_____

Answer the following questions about Yum Yum's prices per pound.

9. What is the mean price for a pound of fudge? _____

10. What is the median price for a pound of fudge? _____

11. What is the range of the prices for a pound of fudge? _____

12. What is the mode of the prices for a pound of fudge? _____

Miles Per Gallon

Use the information provided to answer the questions below.

Justin's car, 15 mpg

Stephen's car, 20 mpg

Drew's car, 30 mpg

Mike's car, 24 mpg

The Smith quadruplets each drove from different colleges to meet up for a ski trip. To get to the ski resort, Justin drove 50 miles fewer than Stephen. Stephen drove for 210 miles to get to the ski resort. Drew drove 110 miles farther than Justin. Mike drove 100 miles farther than Justin to get to the ski resort. How many gallons of gas did each of the Smith brothers use getting to the ski resort? (Round your answers to the nearest tenth.)

1. Justin used _____ gallons of gas.

2. Stephen used _____ gallons of gas.

3. Drew used _____ gallons of gas.

4. Mike used _____ gallons of gas.

Tricky Timing

Which of the following times represent an obtuse angle? For each problem, draw the time shown on each clock.
Then write *yes* or *no* next to each to tell whether its angle is obtuse.
(Note: each measured angle starts at the minute hand and goes clockwise to the hour hand.)

1. 2:33

_____

2. 12:45

_____

3. 3:20

_____

4. 10:42

_____

How many degrees are in the angles formed by the following times? Use a protractor to measure on scrap paper.

5. 1:25

_____

6. 2:53

_____

7. 12:34

_____

8. 9:39

_____

Vote for Meredith!

The school elections are coming up, and Meredith is running for re-election as junior class president. Help Meredith by solving the problems below.

1. Meredith starts by forming an election committee. The ratio of boys to girls is 2:3. If there are 10 people on the committee, how many boys are there? _____

2. The group forms a strategy for the election. They decide to do an informal poll to see how well Meredith might do in the junior class election. Which of these would be the best polling method?

   a. Ask around at a local burger place where a lot of high school students hang out.
   b. Put questionnaires in all student lockers.
   c. Do a secret ballot in 10 randomly selected junior homeroom classes.
   d. Ask everyone who voted for Meredith last year.

3. The poll showed that 40 percent of respondents would definitely vote for her, that 20 percent would definitely not vote for her, and that 40 percent were undecided. If she has only one opponent, does Meredith have a chance to win? Explain. _____

   _____

4. The next step is getting a petition signed so Meredith can be a candidate. Meredith is required to get the signatures of 20% of the junior class. If the junior class is exactly 25% of the whole student body, what percentage of the whole student body will need to sign the petition?

   _____

5. Meredith got her signatures and is officially a candidate. She meets with her committee to begin her campaign. She plans a bake sale to raise money to buy posters and buttons. She decides they will make crispy rice treats and brownies. The ingredients cost her $23.50. They sell 84 brownies for $.75 each and 72 crispy rice treats for $.50 each. After subtracting her costs, how much will she have to spend on her campaign? _____

6. The next stop is the arts and crafts store to buy poster board, markers, and button-making supplies. Supplies for 125 buttons will cost $21.95 plus 6.5% tax. What is the per-unit cost for each button, rounded to the nearest penny? _____

Cargo Calculations

Clyde Cooper loads 8 containers onto a cargo ship. Before the ship can sail, Clyde must record the volume of each. Use the base and height given for each container to calculate its volume. Express your answer in cubic feet. Round your answer to the nearest hundredth.

1.
h = 5 ft
b = 3 ft

_____

2.
h = 4 ft.
b = 2 ft.

_____

3.
h = 2 yds
b = 1 yd

_____

4.
h = 54 in.
b = 36 in.

_____

5.
h = 1 ft
b = 1 ft

_____

6.
h = 8ft
b = 6 ft

_____

7.
h = 4 ft
b = 2.5 ft

_____

8.
h = 66 in
b = 30 in

_____

9. The cargo hold on Clyde's ship can store 400 cubic feet. Can Clyde take all the barrels? _____

10. If Clyde decided to take a smaller ship, with a cargo hold that can store 170 cubic feet, which barrel or barrels should he leave behind? _____

Hot Stuff

Danielle, Jessica, Coby, Drew, and Erika are doing a research project on different countries.
They get together to make a chart of the average temperatures in degrees Celsius for four months. Use the chart to answer the questions below. (Note: the formula to convert temperature Celsius to Fahrenheit is: $C(\frac{9}{5}) + 32$.)

City	January	April	July	October
France	3°C	10°C	19°C	11°C
Greece	9°C	15°C	27°C	18°C
Norway	–5°C	6°C	18°C	6°C
England	5°C	10°C	18°C	13°C
Italy	8°C	14°C	24°C	17°C

1. What formula would you use to convert Fahrenheit to Celsius? _____

2. The average July temperature in Erika's country is 66.2°F. What country is she studying?

_____

3. Drew's country has an average temperature of 80.6°F in the summer. What country is he studying? _____

4. Coby's country is twice as warm in April as it is in January. What country is he studying?

_____

5. Danielle's country has the same average temperature in July as Coby's country. What country is she studying? _____

6. The difference between January and July temperatures in Jessica's country is 28.8°F. What country is she studying? _____

7. Based on the average temperatures, what can you deduce about the geographical location of Danielle's country? _____

8. Which two countries have the most similar temperature averages? _____

Keeping Score

Leah reviewed her test scores from Señora Silvestri's Spanish class. The numerator expresses the number of questions she answered correctly. The denominator expresses the number of questions on the test. Read the test scores in the boxes below. Compare the fractions to determine which test had the highest score each quarter. Express the high score as a percentage.

QUARTER 1

A	$\frac{17}{22}$
B	$\frac{13}{15}$
C	$\frac{4}{5}$
D	$\frac{34}{40}$

1. What was Leah's highest score in Quarter 1? _____

2. Express her high score as a percentage. Round to the nearest whole number. _____

QUARTER 2

A	$\frac{19}{22}$
B	$\frac{27}{30}$
C	$\frac{12}{14}$
D	$\frac{7}{8}$

3. What was Leah's highest score in Quarter 2? _____

4. Express her high score as a percentage. Round to the nearest whole number. _____

QUARTER 3

A	$\frac{28}{33}$
B	$\frac{21}{24}$
C	$\frac{42}{45}$
D	$\frac{5}{6}$

5. What was Leah's highest score in Quarter 3? _____

6. Express her high score as a percentage. Round to the nearest whole number. _____

QUARTER 4

A	$\frac{10}{12}$
B	$\frac{6}{9}$
C	$\frac{22}{27}$
D	$\frac{38}{42}$

7. What was Leah's highest score in Quarter 4? _____

8. Express her high score as a percentage. Round to the nearest whole number. _____

Grand Central Station

Use the train schedule to fill in the missing information below.

Train #	Greenwich	White Plains	Harrison	Chappaqua	Mount Kisco	Redding	Westport	Stamford
10	7:00 AM	7:30	7:45	8:05	8:45	9:30	9:42	9:52
23	7:05 AM	←————————————————— Express —————————————————→						9:22
42	8:12 AM	8:42	8:57	9:17	9:57	10:42	10:54	11:04
77	8:27 AM	8:57	9:12	9:32	10:12	10:57	11:09	11:19
81	9:10 AM	9:40	9:55	10:15	10:55	11:40	11:52	12:02 PM
84	9:30 AM	10:00	10:15	10:35	11:15	12:00 PM	12:12 PM	12:22
95	10:05 AM	10:35	10:50	11:10	11:50	12:35	12:47	12:57
99	10:40 AM	11:10	11:25	11:45	12:25 PM	1:10	1:22	1:32
106	11:17 AM	11:47	12:02 PM	12:22 PM	1:02	1:47	1:59	2:09
118	11:58 AM	12:28 PM	12:43	1:03	1:43	2:28	2:40	2:50

1. Traveler 1 left her hometown and rode the train for 2 hours. When she arrived at her destination, she was about 30 minutes late for a meeting at noon. Traveler 1 left from _____ on train # _____, and arrived in _____.

2. Traveler 2 left earlier than 10 AM. He arrived in Westport 1 hour and 57 minutes later. The train number he is riding on is a multiple of 7 but is not a multiple of 6. Traveler 2 left from _____ on train # _____.

3. Traveler 3 left Greenwich later than 8:30 AM. The trip was 1 hour and 45 minutes long. Traveler 3 arrived at her destination earlier than 11:30 AM. The train number she was on is not divisible by 21. Traveler 3 took train # _____ to _____.

4. Traveler 4 left his hometown later than 11 AM. His train made two stops before reaching its destination. Traveler 4 rode the train for 97 minutes, and he arrived at his destination prior to 1:30 PM. He was not riding train # 95. Traveler 4 left from _____ on train # _____ headed toward _____.

Defining Terms

For each definition below, choose the matching word from the box. Write the answer on the line.

integers	translation
variable	function
inequality	absolute value
reflection	origin

1. The transformation of a figure by sliding it. _____

2. Positive numbers, negative numbers, and zero. _____

3. A letter or symbol representing a varying quantity. _____

4. The transformation of a figure by flipping it. _____

5. The distance a number is from zero on a number line. _____

6. The point at which the *x*-axis and the *y*-axis intersect on a coordinate plane. _____

7. A set of ordered pairs, such as *x*, *y*, in which for each value of *x*, there is only one value of *y*.

_____

8. A number sentence that states that two numbers or quantities are not equal in value.

_____

Bits of Nursery Rhyme Hits

Use the information provided to answer the questions below.

1. *Three blind mice / Three blind mice / See how they run?*

Mouse 1 runs three times as fast as Mouse 2. Mouse 3 runs half as fast as Mouse 1. If Mouse 3 runs at a rate of 6 feet per minute, how fast does Mouse 2 run? _____

2. *Humpty Dumpty sat on a wall / Humpty Dumpty had a great fall*

Humpty Dumpty was taken to the hospital. His bill was $4,530. His insurance covered 70% of his claim, and he had to pay an emergency room fee of $70. If he paid off his bill in 12 equal monthly payments, how much did Humpty have to pay per month? _____

3. *Jack Sprat could eat no fat / His wife could eat no lean*

Jack and Jill Sprat went to a nutritionist to have their body fat percentages measured. Jack weighs 150 pounds and has 5% body fat. Jill weighs 200 pounds and has 25% body fat. What is their average amount of total body fat, expressed as a percentage of the total of their weights? _____

4. *Mary, Mary, quite contrary / How does your garden grow? / With silver bells and cockle shells / And pretty maids all in a row*

Mary wanted to make a cockle shell border for her silver bell flower bed. The bed's circumference is 10 feet. If the shells are $2\frac{1}{4}$ inches wide, and she leaves a space of $\frac{1}{4}$ inch on either side of them, how many shells will she need? _____

5. *Hickory, dickory, dock / The mouse ran up the clock! / The clock struck one / The mouse ran down / Hickory dickory dock*

If the mouse ran up the clock at 10:43 AM and ran down at 1 AM, how many minutes was he inside the clock? _____

6. *The ants go marching eight by eight / The little one stops to shut the gate / And they all go marching down into the ground / To get out of the rain*

If there is a group of ants that is 8 ants deep and 8 ants wide, when the little one shuts the gate, how many ants are still marching down into the ground? _____

7. *All around the mulberry bush / The monkey chased the weasel / The monkey stopped to scratch his nose / Pop, goes the weasel!*

When the monkey scratched his nose, the weasel had his chance! If the circumference of the bush was 18.84 meters, how many meters did the weasel travel through the middle of the bush to escape on the other side? _____

8. *If Peter Piper picked a peck of pickled peppers / How many pickled peppers did Peter Piper pick?*

A pint is equal to $\frac{1}{16}$ of a peck. If there are 33 pickled peppers to a pint, how many pickled peppers did Peter Piper pick? _____

Home to the Chief

Use the information in the box to answer the questions below.

> ## TOP BIRTHPLACES OF U.S. PRESIDENTS
>
> Massachusetts: John Adams, John Quincy Adams, John F. Kennedy, George H. Bush
>
> New York: Martin Van Buren, Millard Fillmore, Theodore Roosevelt, Franklin D. Roosevelt
>
> North Carolina: James Polk, Andrew Johnson
>
> Ohio: Ulysses S. Grant, Rutherford B. Hayes, James Garfield, Benjamin Harrison, William McKinley, William Taft, Warren Harding
>
> Texas: Dwight D. Eisenhower, Lyndon B. Johnson
>
> Vermont: Chester Arthur, Calvin Coolidge
>
> Virginia: George Washington, Thomas Jefferson, James Madison, James Monroe, William Henry Harrison, John Tyler, Zachary Taylor, Woodrow Wilson

1. Which state was home to the most presidents? _____

2. How many U.S. presidents were born in each of the 7 states listed above? List states in order of most to least.

_____

_____

3. Draw a bar graph that represents the information shown in the chart above.

4. What is the mean number of U.S. presidents born in each of the 7 states listed? Round your answer to the nearest tenth. _____

5. What is the median number of U.S. presidents per state? _____

Market Measure

Marina is at the grocery store, but the weights on the food are all in kilograms! Use the formula in the box and your knowledge of conversions to help Marina determine how much she is buying. Round your answers to the nearest hundredth.

1 kg = 2.204 lb

1. 0.2 kg American cheese = _____ lb

2. 2 kg chicken cutlet = _____ lb

3. 2.9 kg ground beef = _____ lb

4. 0.5 kg button mushrooms = _____ lb

5. 1.2 kg tomatoes = _____ lb

6. 3 kg onions = _____ lb

7. 1.3 kg turkey = _____ lb

8. 2.27 kg red potatoes = _____ lb

9. 1.75 kg watermelon = _____ lb

10. 0.75 kg cucumbers = _____ lb

Conversion Chase

Find a stopwatch or a clock with a second hand. Read the questions, and provide the conversions requested below. Use the timer to see how long it takes you to answer all of the questions. Try the questions again and see if you can beat your time. Cover your answers to the first race with a sheet of paper.

Race 1

1. 1 yard = _____ feet

2. 1 foot = _____ inches

3. 1 mile = _____ feet

4. 1 kilogram = _____ pounds

5. 1 pound = _____ ounces

6. 1 ton = _____ pounds

7. 1 centimeter = _____ meters

8. 1 kilometer = _____ millimeters

9. 1 cup = _____ fluid ounces

10. 1 pint = _____ cups

11. 1 quart = _____ pints

12. 1 gallon = _____ quarts

Race 2

1. 1 yard = _____ feet

2. 1 foot = _____ inches

3. 1 mile = _____ feet

4. 1 kilogram = _____ pounds

5. 1 pound = _____ ounces

6. 1 ton = _____ pounds

7. 1 centimeter = _____ meters

8. 1 kilometer = _____ millimeters

9. 1 cup = _____ fluid ounces

10. 1 pint = _____ cups

11. 1 quart = _____ pints

12. 1 gallon = _____ quarts

Listen Longer

The Mason Brothers released their debut CD, *Meet the Masons*. Use the chart to answer the questions below.

Track	Time
1	7:13
2	4:55
3	6:04
4	6:12
5	5:39
6	4:22
7	4:04
8	3:11
9	3:49
10	4:36
11	4:55
12	6:00

1. What is the total running time of the CD? _____

2. Delia downloaded every song shorter than 5:00. If each download cost $0.99, how much did she spend? _____

3. What percentage of the CD's songs are longer than 6:10? Round your answer to the nearest whole number. _____

4. Adriano downloaded the fifth-longest track. Which track did he download? _____

5. What is the median song length on the Mason Brothers album? _____

6. What is the mode for song lengths on the Mason Brothers album? _____

7. What is the range of song lengths on the Mason Brothers album? _____

8. What is the mean song length on the Mason Brothers album? _____

9. How do you think Track 1 affects the mean? Explain. _____

_____

10. How do you think Track 8 affects the mean? Explain. _____

_____

Hoops Help

Use the diagram to answer the questions below.

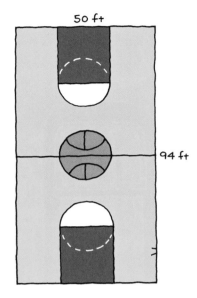

50 ft

94 ft

1. Hillside High School's basketball court needs a new coat of varnish. What is the area of the floor that needs to be covered? _____

2. Each quart of varnish covers 60 square feet. How many quarts are needed to finish the floor?

_____

3. There are four quarts in a gallon. A quart of varnish costs $12. Gallons of varnish are 2 for $70. Is it cheaper to buy the varnish by the gallon or by the quart? _____

4. The basketball team is holding a raffle to pay for the varnish. How much money do they need to earn? _____

5. Raffle tickets cost $1.25 each. How many do they need to sell to reach their goal? _____

6. The school must rope off the perimeter of the floor while the varnish dries. How long should the rope be? _____

7. The Hillside Hornets have a record of 29 wins and 25 losses this season. What is their winning percentage? Round your answer to the nearest whole number. _____

8. Last season the team had a record of 40 wins and 37 losses. Does the team have a better record this season or last season? _____

Fill 'Er Up!

Use the information provided to answer the questions below.

1. Aaron's car gets 28 miles per gallon of gasoline. How much gasoline will he burn in 140 miles?

_____

2. Tia's car gets 32 miles per gallon. How far can she travel on 3.5 gallons of gas? _____

3. Josh drives a hybrid car that gets 48 miles per gallon. How much gasoline will he burn in 240 miles? _____

4. How much better is Josh's gas mileage than Aaron's? Express your answer as a percentage.

_____

5. Linnea gets 35 miles per gallon. Her gas tank has a capacity of 13.5 gallons. How far can she travel on one tank of gas? _____

6. Jordan's truck gets 26 miles per gallon. His gas tank holds 16.5 gallons. How far can he travel on a $\frac{1}{4}$ tank of gas? _____

7. Gas costs $4.06 per gallon. How much did Jordan spend to fill his tank from empty? _____

8. Gas costs $3.96 per gallon. Linnea spent $48.51. How much gas did she buy? _____

Mountain High, Valley Low

Use the list of mountain heights below to complete the graph and answer the questions.

Mountain	Height (ft)
Mt. Vancouver	15,979
Mt. Bear	14,831
Mt. McKinley	20,320
South Buttress	15,885
Mt. Blackburn	16,390
University Peak	14,470
Mt. Fairweather	15,300
Browne Tower	14,530
Mt. St. Elias	18,008
Mt. Churchill	15,638
Mt. Foraker	17,400
Mt. Bona	16,500

1. Place the mountains in order from shortest to tallest.

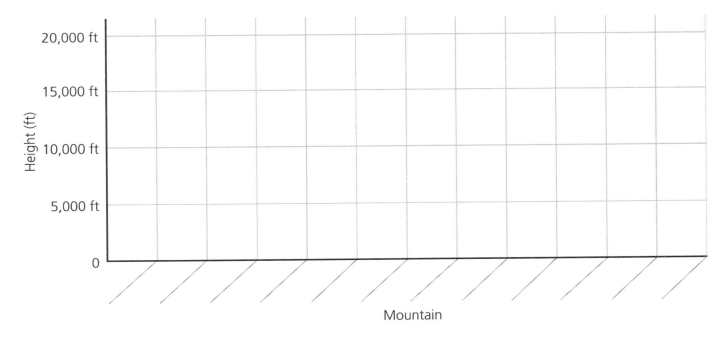

2. Calculate the mean height on the graph. _____

3. Calculate the median height on the graph. _____

4. All of these mountains are in which U.S. state? _____

Snack Savvy

Sari is doing a report about one of her favorite snack foods, Chee-Zees, which come in a two-cup bag. Use the nutrition label below to help her answer the questions that will follow. Assume that Sari eats 2,000 calories per day.

```
┌─────────────────────────────────────────────────────────────┐
│ Nutrition Facts                                               │
│ Serving Size 1 cup (228g)                                     │
│ Servings Per Container 2                                      │
├───────────────────────────────────────────────────────────── │
│ Amount Per Serving                                            │
├─────────────────────────────────────────────────────────────┤
│ Calories 280                        Calories from Fat 120     │
├─────────────────────────────────────────────────────────────┤
│                                          % Daily Value*       │
│ Total Fat 13g                                        20%      │
│ Saturated Fat 5g                                     25%      │
│ Trans Fat 2g                                                  │
│ Cholesterol 2mg                                      10%      │
│ Sodium 660mg                                         28%      │
│ Total Carbohydrate 31g                               10%      │
│ Dietary Fiber 3g                                      0%      │
│ Sugars 5g                                                     │
│ Protein 5g                                                    │
│ Vitamin A 4%            •          Vitamin C 2%               │
│ Calcium 15%                        Iron 4%                    │
├─────────────────────────────────────────────────────────────┤
│ *Percent Daily Values are based on a 2,000-calorie diet. Your │
│ daily values may be higher or lower depending on your calorie │
│ needs.                                                        │
│                    Calories:   2,000        2,500            │
│ Total Fat        Less than     65g          80g              │
│ Sat Fat          Less than     20g          25g              │
│ Cholesterol      Less than     300mg        300mg            │
│ Sodium           Less than     2,400mg      2,400mg          │
│ Total Carbohydrate             300g         375g             │
│ Fiber                          25g          30g              │
├─────────────────────────────────────────────────────────────┤
│ Calories Per Gram:                                            │
│ Fat 9        •    Carbohydrate 4    •    Protein 4           │
└─────────────────────────────────────────────────────────────┘
```

1. Sari was surprised to learn that a small bag of Chee-Zees contains two servings but that the calorie count on the bag is for only one serving. What percentage of her daily calories are in one full bag of Chee-Zees? _____

2. Sari eats one bag of Chee-Zees with her lunch. Based on the daily recommendations for sodium on the label, what percentage of her daily sodium intake has she eaten in this snack? _____

3. What is the proportion of saturated fat in a bag of Chee-Zees to the recommended daily value of saturated fat for Sari's 2,000-calorie diet? Express your answer as a fraction. _____

4. What percentage of the total calories in Chee-Zees is from fat? Round your answer to the nearest tenth. _____

5. An adequate intake (AI) of daily fiber for young women is 25 grams. If Sari eats a serving of this snack, what percentage of her AI will she have eaten? _____

6. How many bags of Chee-Zees would Sari have to eat to get a full day's worth of calcium? Round your answer to the nearest tenth. _____

Sweet Victory

To answer the sticky riddle in the box, solve the problems below to determine the value of *n*.
Using the key at the bottom of the page, find the letter that matches your numeric answer.
Mark that letter in the square to the right of each question. Read from top to bottom to answer the riddle!

> Riddle: Why did Honey B. Hive win the election?

1. $7n + 3 = 52$ _____ ☐

2. $\dfrac{4}{8} \times \dfrac{24}{n} = 6$ _____ ☐

3. $60\% = \dfrac{n}{5}$ _____ ☐

4. $13n - 6^2 = -10$ _____ ☐

5. $2^3 \times -2n = -64$ _____ ☐

6. $(3^3 - 18) \div n = 1$ _____ ☐

7. $25 \times 0.20 = n$ _____ ☐

8. $93 - 7n = 37$ _____ ☐

9. $4\dfrac{1}{2} \div \dfrac{1}{4} = n$ _____ ☐

10. 30% of $60 = n$ _____ ☐

2 = H	4 = A
3 = E	5 = B
7 = S	8 = U
9 = D	18 = Z

Let's Mush!

Using the chart and the information provided below, answer the following questions about Alaska's Iditarod dog sled race.

IDITAROD RACE

Team	Number of Days to Complete Iditarod
A	20
B	18
C	9
D	10
E	10
F	11
G	14

1. What was the mean number of days it took the teams to complete the race? Round your answer to the nearest whole number. _____

2. What was the median number of days it took the teams to complete the race? _____

3. What was the mode number of days it took the teams to complete the race? _____

4. What is the range for the number of days it took the teams to complete the race? _____

5. The length of the Iditarod is about 1,150 miles. How many feet is that? _____

6. If a team completes the race in 16 days, what was the average number of miles traveled per day?

_____

7. The ceremonial starting point of the Iditarod is Anchorage, Alaska. The ending point is Nome, Alaska. Anchorage has a population of about 282,813. Nome has a population of about 3,505. How much larger is Anchorage's population? Express your answer as a percentage. _____

8. Last year, 78 teams raced. If 51 teams had 16 dogs, and 27 teams had 12 dogs, how many dogs were in the race? _____

Writing Inequalities

Write a story that matches the inequality shown. The first one is done for you.

1. $x < 25$

Martin ran on the treadmill at the gym today for 25 minutes. Maggie also ran on the treadmill today, but not for as long as Martin did. The inequality describes how long Maggie ran on the treadmill.

2. $x \geq 4$

_____

_____

_____

3. $x < -7$

_____

_____

_____

4. $x \geq 45$

_____

_____

_____

5. $x \leq 30$

_____

_____

_____

Orchard Outing

Ten friends went apple picking at Orville's Orchard. Use the chart to answer the following questions about their day at the orchard.

Name	Number of Apples
Avish	17
Jemma	27
Daniela	17
Young	9
Jamina	22
Nick	16
Chloe	11
Mairead	21
Kevin	17
Chen	23

1. How many apples did the friends pick? _____

2. What was the mean number of apples picked? _____

3. What was the median number of apples picked? _____

4. What was the mode number of apples picked? _____

5. What was the range of the number of apples picked? _____

6. Which pair picked more apples: Kevin and Jamina or Chloe and Jemma? _____

7. It costs $8 a bag to pick apples. There are 12 apples in a bag. How much did the friends pay in total? _____

8. It takes $2\frac{1}{2}$ pounds of apples to make a pie. The apples weigh about 8 oz each. How many apples are needed for 2 pies? _____

Pizzeria Pitchers

Use the pictures and the information in the box to solve the problems below.

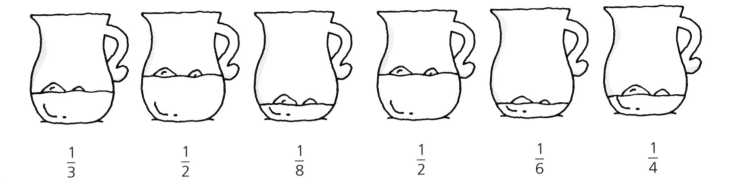

$\frac{1}{3}$ $\frac{1}{2}$ $\frac{1}{8}$ $\frac{1}{2}$ $\frac{1}{6}$ $\frac{1}{4}$

On Saturday night, the pizzeria offered sweet tea and fruit punch as its specialty drinks. The pitchers pictured show how much sweet tea and fruit punch were left over at the end of the night. There were three pitchers with leftover sweet tea and three pitchers with leftover fruit punch. Two of the pitchers had the same amount of liquid left in them—one of those pitchers contained sweet tea while the other contained fruit punch. The pitcher with the least amount of liquid contained sweet tea. One of the leftover pitchers of fruit punch was $\frac{1}{3}$ full. That pitcher was twice as full as another pitcher of fruit punch. As the busboy cleaned up, he poured all the leftover sweet tea into a plastic pitcher. He poured all the leftover fruit punch into a glass pitcher.

1. After the cleanup, how much liquid was in the plastic pitcher?

_____

2. After the cleanup, how much liquid was in the glass pitcher?

_____

It's Outta There!

The Tinytown Little League has just finished its fall season. Use the chart to answer the questions below.

Team	Wins	Losses	Runs Scored	Runs Allowed
Cougars	11	3	42	9
Lions	11	4	40	12
Panthers	10	5	35	16
Cheetahs	7	8	32	23
Tigers	7	8	29	25
Wildcats	4	10	11	32

1. Which team had the highest percentage of wins compared to total games played?

_____

2. Which team allowed exactly half the runs of another team? _____

3. Why are the Cheetahs ranked above the Tigers, even though they won and lost the same number of games? _____

_____

4. Which team scored an average of 1.93 runs per game? _____

5. Which team scored 88% of the runs that the Lions did? _____

The Pythagorean Expectation (also known as PCT) is a number statisticians use to predict the percentage of games a baseball team is likely to win in the future, or "win percentage." Use the formula to calculate the PCT for each team in the Tinytown Little League (rounded to the nearest hundredth), and convert them to percentages.

> The formula to calculate PCT:
>
> Win percentage = Runs Scored^2 ÷ (Runs Scored^2 + Runs Allowed^2)

6. Cougars

_____

7. Lions

_____

8. Panthers

_____

9. Cheetahs

_____

10. Tigers

_____

11. Wildcats

_____

12. What is the average number of runs scored by all the teams combined for the season?

_____

Mercury Rising

Use the chart to answer the questions below.

AVERAGE MONTHLY TEMPERATURES FOR ASWAN, EGYPT

Month	Temperature	Month	Temperature
January	70°F	July	103°F
February	74°F	August	102°F
March	82°F	September	98°F
April	92°F	October	93°F
May	99°F	November	80°F
June	103°F	December	72°F

1. On average, what is the coldest month in Aswan? _____

2. On average, what are the hottest months in Aswan? _____

3. What is the mean temperature in Aswan? _____

4. What is the median temperature in Aswan? _____

5. What is the mode temperature in Aswan? _____

6. What is the range of temperatures on the chart above? _____

7. The average temperature in Miami, Florida, in May is 31° Celsius. Which city experiences higher temperatures in May: Miami or Aswan? _____

8. Draw a bar graph that charts the average monthly temperatures in Aswan, Egypt.

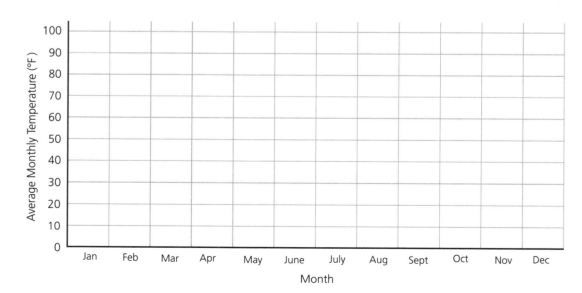

The Stew Stop

Solve the word problems about the Sayville Stew Stop.

1. Sally is the head chef at Sayville's most popular lunch destination, The Stew Stop. To make her famous stew, Sally uses 1 lb of potatoes, $\frac{3}{4}$ lb of ground beef, $\frac{2}{3}$ cup of carrots, and $1\frac{1}{2}$ teaspoons of salt. But, Sally's sous chef accidentally added too much salt to the recipe today! If the sous chef added 3 extra teaspoons of salt to the stew, how much of the other ingredients should Sally add to make the recipe right again? _____

_____

_____

_____

2. The Stew Stop has been the victim of a number of robberies recently. Someone has been stealing Sally's secret recipes. Sayville's chief of police is determined to catch the burglar once and for all. The sous chef is always the last person in the restaurant each night. Sally is always the first person in the restaurant each morning. Both Sally and the sous chef have reported seeing the robber, but he looks different each time! The robber is always wearing some sort of hat: a beret, a baseball hat, or a winter hat. He also always wears fake facial hair: either a beard or a moustache. In addition to the hat and facial hair, the robber also always wears a scarf: red, green, or orange. How many different possible disguises is the robber using? Remember, he is always wearing a hat, scarf, and fake facial hair. _____

Patrolling the Perimeter

Using the information provided, give the perimeter of the shapes described below.

1. An octagon that is 81 feet on each side. _____

2. A trapezoid with sides measuring 11.3 meters, 5.6 meters, 16.0 meters, and 6.5 meters.

_____

3. A square with an area of 225 square feet. _____

4. A rectangle that is three times longer than it is wide and has an area of 432 square meters.

_____

5. A rhombus with a base of 20.4 meters and a height of 17.1 meters.

_____

6. A rectangle with a base of 18.1 feet and a height of 30.7 feet. _____

7. A kite with two sides measuring 29.9 feet and two sides measuring 26.3 feet. _____

8. A quadrilateral with four 90° angles and equal sides. One side is 2,640 feet. Express your answer in miles. _____

Go Long!

Circle the best answer for the following questions about length.

1. Which is longer?

    a. A traffic jam that is 2 miles long

    b. A traffic jam that is 5 kilometers long

2. Which animal traveled farther?

    a. The grasshopper that jumped 2.1 inches

    b. The beetle that crawled 4.5 centimeters

3. Which is longer?

    a. A football field that is 360 feet long

    b. An Olympic-sized pool that is 50 meters long

4. Who ran farther?

    a. Tess, who ran 100 yards

    b. Ellie, who ran 100 meters

5. Which state is longer?

    a. Nebraska, which is 690 kilometers long

    b. Kansas, which is 417 miles long

6. Which state is wider?

    a. Delaware, at 30 miles wide

    b. Rhode Island, at 60 kilometers wide

7. Which is longer?

    a. A goldfish that is 6.2 centimeters long

    b. An earthworm that is 2.7 inches long

8. Which suspension bridge is higher?

    a. Golden Gate Bridge, at 220 feet

    b. Verrazano-Narrows Bridge, at 69 meters

Lucky Day

The Lucktown Little League is holding its annual raffle. There are 800 tickets being sold. Use the information provided to answer the questions below. Reduce your answers to lowest terms.

1. If all the tickets are sold, what is the probability of winning any of the prizes? _____

2. What is the probability of winning a cash prize? _____

3. What is the probability of winning the television if you buy 20 tickets? _____

4. What is the probability of winning a movie pass if you buy one raffle ticket? _____

5. Bessie Bennett plays bingo every Tuesday night at the Lucktown Recreation Center. Tonight, 36 people are playing. Each player is playing with 3 bingo cards. What are Bessie's odds of winning?

_____

6. After a break, a new game of bingo begins. This time, 14 players use 2 bingo cards and 25 players use 3 bingo cards. What is the probability that Bessie will win if she uses 3 cards?

_____

7. There are still 36 people at the bingo game. If there are 4 women named Bessie playing bingo tonight, and they all have the same number of cards, what are the odds that a woman named Bessie will shout, "BINGO!"? _____

Verifying the Facts

For each problem, determine if the answer is correct. Write *yes* or *no* on the line.
If it is not correct, write the correct answer.

1. Marvin has 25 first cousins. If there are 26 bones in a human foot, how many bones are in the feet of Marvin and his cousins?

   Answer: 676 bones _____

2. For his daily walk, Marvin walks around the perimeter of his yard 10 times. The yard is 30 feet by 40 feet. How far does Marvin walk each day?

   Answer: 1,600 feet _____

3. The five brothers McMullin ate 80 slices of pizza in 12 minutes! What is the average number of slices of pizza each brother ate per minute?

   Answer: 1.3 slices of pizza _____

4. The brothers McMullin are eating again, especially Brian McMullin. Brian ate 3.7 pounds of steak every day for 10 days. How much steak would he eat if he did that three times this month?

   Answer: 119 pounds _____

5. Big Bob outweighs Small Paul by 6 times. But, amazingly, Small Paul can lift up Big Bob, and then some! Today, Big Bob was holding an 80-pound weight when Small Paul picked him up. Small Paul was lifting a total of 410 pounds! How much does Small Paul weigh?

   Answer: 55 pounds _____

6. Big Bob and Small Paul work out at the same gym. Today, Big Bob lifted 203 pounds and Small Paul lifted 174 pounds. What ratio describes the comparison of Bob's lifts to Paul's lifts, in lowest terms?

   Answer: $\frac{8}{9}$ _____

Birthday Surprise

Use the information provided to answer the questions below.

Aidan's grandfather is celebrating his 82nd birthday. Aidan bought 82 balloons for Grandpa Green's surprise birthday party. Four balloons popped when Aidan took the balloons out of the car. The remaining balloons are four different colors. Twelve are blue. Three are yellow. The rest are purple or green. Green is Grandpa's favorite color, so there are twice as many green balloons as there are purple balloons.

1. How many balloons did Grandpa Green receive? _____

2. How many green balloons are there? _____

3. How many purple balloons are there? _____

4. How many red balloons are there? _____

5. What color were the four balloons that popped? _____

6. Aidan's cousin, Connor, brought Grandpa Green an additional 26 balloons. One is yellow and four are blue. There are twice as many green balloons as purple ones. How many green balloons did Connor bring? _____

7. Each guest went home with two of the balloons that Aidan and Connor brought. Grandpa Green kept 10 for himself. How many guests attended the party? _____

8. Draw a bar graph that shows the total amount of balloons that Grandpa Green received from Aidan and Connor combined.

Strategizing

For each problem, circle the problem-solving strategy that would allow you to determine the answer.

1. If Champ runs for .25 hour and covers a distance of 5 miles, at what rate (in mph) is Champ running?

    a. Translate to a ratio.
    b. Use mental math.
    c. Use trial and error.

2. The student is 62 inches tall. Is this the same as 5 feet tall?

    a. Translate to a ratio.
    b. Draw a diagram.
    c. Use mental math.

3. If a Supercar 2000 won 4 of the last 13 car races, at this rate, how many will Supercar 2000 win in the next 65 races?

    a. Estimate.
    b. Make a number line.
    c. Translate to a proportion.

4. There are 2,500 patrons at a Broadway musical performance. They are seated in 6 sets of seats. If 5 of the 6 sets of seats hold the same amount, and the 6th set of seats holds 12 times that amount, how many patrons are seated in the first 5 sets of seats?

    a. Translate to a proportion.
    b. Write an equation.
    c. Estimate.

5. Beagle and Dalmation have each won Best in Show at the dog show several times in the past five years. You want to compare their wins during that time.

    a. Make a graph.
    b. Make a number line.
    c. Use trial and error.

6. Each moving box in the storage space is 1 cubic foot. The storage space has 425 cubic feet of space. How many boxes will fit in the storage space?

    a. Use trial and error.
    b. Estimate.
    c. Make a number line.

7. Track Star 3 is ahead of Track Star 2, who is three places behind Track Star 6. Track Star 1 is 2 places ahead of Track Star 4, who is 2 places ahead of Track Star 5. Who is closet to the finish line?

    a. Write an equation.
    b. Translate to a proportion.
    c. Draw a diagram.

8. You know what time 6 school physicals begin, and how long each physical takes. How can you arrange for 24 students to have physicals at different times?

    a. Make a chart.
    b. Make a number line.
    c. Use trial and error.

Scheduling Dilemma

Use the information provided to make up a train schedule that fits the criteria below.

Train #	Manhasset	Mineola	Patchogue	Port Jefferson	Roslyn	Sayville	Seaford
11							
14							
24							
30							
32							
45							
61							
75							

🚂 Trains stop in all cities.

🚂 The time between cities is the same for all trains.

🚂 Lower number trains leave before higher number trains.

🚂 No trains leave any city at the same time.

🚂 The time between Roslyn and Seaford is 35 minutes.

🚂 Trains with numbers divisible by 2 leave Manhasset between 8 AM and 11 AM.

🚂 Trains with numbers divisible by 3 leave Manhasset at 5 minutes after the hour.

🚂 The time between Sayville and Seaford is 15 minutes.

Box Score Battle

Use the chart to answer the following questions about a baseball game
between the Youngtown Yaks and the Mayville Manatees.

Box Score	1	2	3	4	5	6	7	8	9	R	H	E
Youngtown Yaks	0	0	6	0	0	?	0	2	0	12	?	2
Mayville Manatees	?	0	0	1	0	0	1	0	3	6	12	0

Key: R = Runs; H = Hits; E = Errors

1. How many runs did the Yaks score in the 6th inning? _____

2. How many runs did the Manatees score in the 1st inning? _____

3. The ratio of Youngtown Yaks hits to Mayville Manatees hits could be expressed as 3:2. How many
hits did the Yaks get? _____

4. The Yaks got $\frac{2}{3}$ of their hits in the 3rd inning. How many hits did they get in that inning? _____

5. What was the mean number of runs per inning for the Yaks? _____

6. What was the median number of runs per inning for the Manatees? _____

7. What was the mode of the runs per inning for the Yaks? _____

8. The Manatees had a win-loss ratio of 30:59 going into today's game. What is their new win-loss
ratio? Express your answer as a decimal. Round to the nearest thousandth. _____

Big Birds

Answer the following birdbrained questions.

1. An ostrich and an emu stand next to each other. The emu is 200 centimeters. The ostrich is 84 inches. Which bird is larger? _____

2. Each eyeball of an ostrich, the largest of any bird, measures 2 inches across. Assuming an ostrich has round eyes, what is each eye's radius? _____ What is each eye's circumference?

_____

3. Emperor penguin chicks weigh 318 grams when they hatch. Express the weight as kilograms.

_____

4. An ostrich can run 50 miles per hour. How quickly can an ostrich run a quarter mile at full speed? Express your answer in seconds. _____

5. An emperor penguin will walk 50 miles to get to its nesting site. Express this number in feet.

_____

6. A peacock's distinctive train of tail feathers can measure 5 feet long. The tail feathers account for 60% of the peacock's length. How long is a peacock without its tail feathers? Round your answer to the nearest tenth. _____

7. A bald eagle's wingspan is $\frac{2}{3}$ the size of a California condor's wingspan. A bald eagle has a wingspan of 6 feet. What is a California condor's wingspan? _____

8. In the 1960s there were only about 400 breeding pairs of bald eagles in the contiguous United States. Today there are about 6,000 breeding pairs. By what percentage has the population of breeding pairs grown since the 1960s? _____

Reduce, Reuse, Recycle

Use the information in the box to answer the questions below.

Two couples—Jaclyn and Shareef, and Susie and Chris—are making an effort to live green. They collected glass and plastic bottles to be recycled. Together, they brought a total of 177 bottles to the recycling center. Each person had the same number of bottles in each of their individual canvas bags, but that number differed from person to person. Altogether, the green couples filled 24 canvas bags. Jaclyn and Chris filled the same number of bags. Together, Shareef and Susie filled 12 bags. Shareef and Chris collected the same number of bottles. Shareef filled 2 more bags than Susie. Together, Jaclyn and Susie collected 9 more bottles than Shareef and Chris combined. Each person collected somewhere between 40 and 50 bottles.

1. How many bags did each person fill?

_____

_____

_____

_____

2. How many bottles were in each of their bags?

_____

_____

_____

_____

3. Which couple collected the most bottles?

_____

Fruity Findings

There are 80 students in Mrs. Plum's class. They took a poll to see what fruits the students like best. Use the pie chart to solve the problems below.

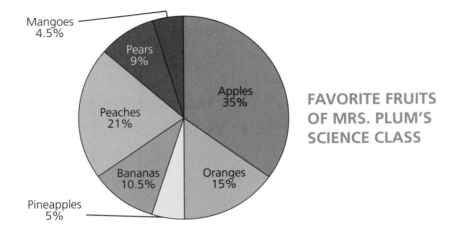

FAVORITE FRUITS OF MRS. PLUM'S SCIENCE CLASS

1. What is the most popular fruit among students in Mrs. Plum's science class? _____

2. What is the second most popular fruit? _____

3. How many students prefer apples? _____

4. How many prefer oranges? _____

5. How many students prefer fruit that starts with the letter *P*? _____

6. Create a pie chart with the following data for all of the students at Appleton Middle School: 45% prefer apples; 12.5% prefer peaches; 12.5% prefer bananas; 10% prefer oranges; 10% prefer pears; 5% prefer mangoes; 5% prefer pineapples.

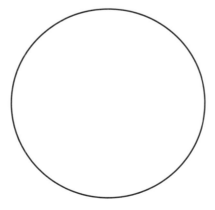

7. There are 500 students at Appleton Middle School. How many of them prefer apples? _____

8. How many prefer a fruit other than apples or oranges? _____

Measure for Measure

Solve the problems below.

1. 2 pounds, 3 ounces − 1 pound, 13 ounces = _____

2. 6 pounds, 12 ounces + 7 pounds, 7 ounces = _____

3. 3 yards, 1 foot − 2 yards, 2 feet = _____

4. 5 yards, 2 feet + 7 yards, 2 feet = _____

5. 5 feet, 3 inches − 3 feet, 8 inches = _____

6. 7 feet, 9 inches + 12 feet, 5 inches = _____

7. 2 meters, 18 centimeters − 1 meter, 97 centimeters = _____

8. 4 centimeters, 9 millimeters + 7 centimeters, 2 millimeters = _____

9. 5 metric tons, 950 pounds − 1 metric ton, 20 pounds = _____

10. 1 gram, 450 milligrams + 8 grams, 600 milligrams = _____

11. 8 pints − 7 pints, 1 cup = _____

12. 3 gallons, 2 quarts + 2 gallons, 3 quarts = _____

123

Working for the Weekend

Tom is making extra money this summer mowing lawns. He has been hired by his neighbor,
Mr. Lowry, to mow the lawn and do other tasks around the yard. Use the map of the Lowry's property,
measured in feet, to solve the following problems about Tom's job.

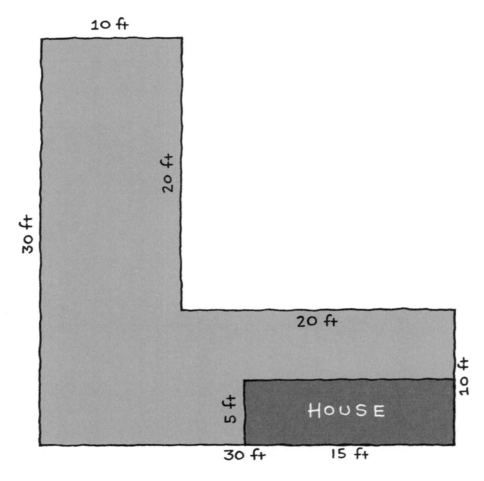

1. Tom estimates he can mow 100 square feet every 30 minutes. How many hours would it take to mow the lawn? _____

2. Mr. Lowry agrees to pay Tom $6.20 per hour. How much can he expect to make mowing the lawn? _____

3. For the same pay rate, Tom could also trim the outer edges of the lawn. If he can trim two yards of edging every four minutes, how much extra pay can he earn? _____

4. The gutters on the front edge of the house also need to be cleaned. Mr. Lowry offers a 50% pay bonus to Tom for this task. If he completes the cleaning in 1.5 hours, how much extra pay can he expect? _____

5. Here is the invoice Tom prepared for Mr. Lowry. Fill in the blanks with time, rate, cost, and grand total.

```
┌─────────────────────────────────────────────────────────────┐
│                      I N V O I C E                            │
├─────────────────────────────────────────────────────────────┤
│  Mr. Al Lowry                                                 │
│  33 Sunshine Street                                           │
│  ┌──────────────┬──────────────┬──────────┬──────────────┐   │
│  │ Lawn Mowing  │ ____ Hours   │ × $____  │ = $____      │   │
│  │ Edge Trimming│ ____ Hours   │ × $____  │ = $____      │   │
│  │ Gutter Cleaning│ ____ Hours │ × $____  │ = $____      │   │
│  └──────────────┴──────────────┴──────────┴──────────────┘   │
│                              GRAND TOTAL  │ $           │     │
└─────────────────────────────────────────────────────────────┘
```

6. Mr. Lowry would like to put up a fence around the edge of his property. If the fencing comes in nine-foot rolls, how many rolls would he have to buy? _____

7. The gardening store is having a 20%-off sale on fencing this week. If Mr. Lowry paid $472 for the fencing (before tax and delivery), what was the original price per roll? _____

8. If the sales tax is 6%, and the delivery fee for the fencing is $1.25 per roll, what is the total price Mr. Lowry paid for the fencing including tax and delivery? (Note: sales tax does not apply to services, such as delivery.) _____

9. The following year, Tom raises his rates for lawn care. He is now making $7.00 per hour. Because Tom knows the property well, he can now mow the lawn in 4 hours. How much will he make for each 15 minutes it takes him to mow the lawn? _____

10. By the time Tom is out of college, he runs his own lawn care business. His lawn mowing service charges $10.00 as a basic fee, plus $2 for every 500 square feet mowed. Express the total charges (C) as a function of square feet (m) mowed. _____

Movie Madness

Anna, Ian, David, Carly, and Nick are spending a Saturday afternoon at the movie theater.
Using the information provided, fill in the chart indicating what snack each person ate at the movies.

Clues:

- Each person got a different treat.
- Carly got the jelly beans.
- Ian is sitting between the person who got the hot pretzel and Anna.
- The person sitting in the first seat got nachos.
- David is in the third seat.
- The person who got popcorn is three seats to Nick's right.

	Popcorn	Hot Pretzel	Chocolate Bar	Jelly Beans	Nachos
Anna					
Ian					
David					
Carly					
Nick					

Now, write the order in which the friends were seated.

1. _____

2. _____

3. _____

4. _____

5. _____

Road Trip!

Use the information provided to answer the questions below.

1. Dave Driver and his sister Dory are going on a road trip. The first stop is their uncle Frank's house in Millville. Uncle Frank's house is 40 minutes away. If they travel 42 miles per hour, how many miles away does he live? _____

2. Uncle Frank isn't home. Aunt Dorothy says he has gone to the Donut Shack for breakfast. Dave and Dory drive at a speed of 30 miles per hour. They arrive at the Donut Shack in 10 minutes. How far is the Donut Shack? _____

3. The next stop on the trip is the Seven Hills theme park. The park opens at 9:00 AM. If the park is 60 miles away and they travel 50 miles per hour, what time should Dave and Dory leave to get to the park the minute it opens? _____

4. Dave and Dory leave the park at 4:00 PM and travel 20 miles to Grandma and Grandpa Driver's house. They drive 50 miles per hour. What time do they arrive? _____

5. After they wash up, Dave and Dory decide to go for a run. Dory runs 5 miles in 50 minutes. How many miles per hour did she run? _____

6. Dave ran 4 miles in 42 minutes. Who ran faster—Dave or Dory? _____

7. Dory buys gas. Gas costs $3.85 per gallon. She pays $50.05. How much gas does she buy?

_____

8. Dory and Dave drive home. If they return home exactly the way they came and at the same speed, how long will the trip take them? _____

Can't Win 'Em All

Use the information in the chart to answer the questions below.

FOOTBALL CONFERENCE STANDINGS

Team	Wins	Losses	Points For	Points Against
A	7	1	227	114
B	6	2	208	111
C	5	3	223	143
D	5	3	203	151
E	4	4	166	189
F	4	4	142	177
G	3	5	111	159
H	1	7	123	263

1. How many more points did Team A score than Team F? _____

2. How many more points did other teams score against Team G than Team C? _____

3. What was Team B's winning percentage? _____

4. What was Team H's winning percentage? _____

5. What was the range of "points for"? _____

6. What was the range of "points against"? _____

7. Which team had the highest ratio of "points for" to "points against"? _____

8. Which team had the lowest ratio of "points for" to "points against"? _____

Window Box Wonders

Poppy Green needs soil for her rectangular window boxes. Using the lengths, widths, and heights provided, calculate the volume of the window boxes below. Then answer the questions using the information provided.

1.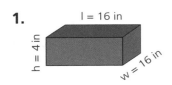

l = 16 in
h = 4 in
w = 16 in

_____

2.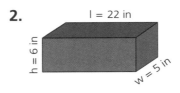

l = 22 in
h = 6 in
w = 5 in

_____

3.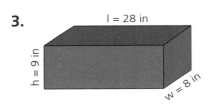

l = 28 in
h = 9 in
w = 8 in

_____

4.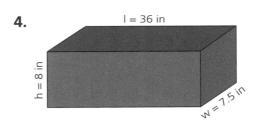

l = 36 in
h = 8 in
w = 7.5 in

_____

5.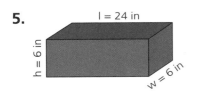

l = 24 in
h = 6 in
w = 6 in

_____

6.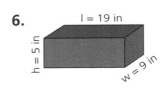

l = 19 in
h = 5 in
w = 9 in

_____

7. What is the total amount of soil Poppy will need to fill all of the window boxes? Give your answer in cubic feet and round it to the nearest whole number. (Hint: divide the total cubic inches by 12^3.) _____

8. When Poppy arrives at the garden store, she sees that pots of red poppies are on sale, 4 for $19.99. If she buys two pots of poppies for each window box, how much will she spend?

_____

Frisbee Frenzy

Use the frisbees to answer the questions below.

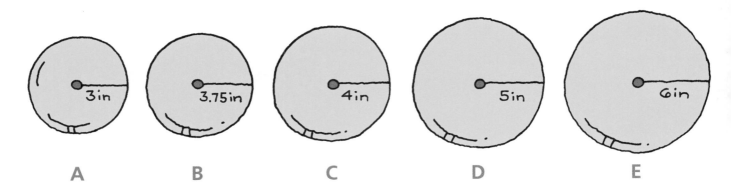

| A | B | C | D | E |

1. Frank Spinner's lucky Frisbee has a diameter of 7.5 inches. Which one is it? _____

2. Carlotta Spinner's favorite Frisbee has an area of 113.04 square inches. Which one is it? _____

3. Izzy Turner borrowed her cousin's Frisbee for today's practice. It has a diameter of 20.32 centimeters. Which one is it? _____

4. What is the area of Izzy's borrowed Frisbee in centimeters? Round your answer to the nearest whole number. _____

5. What is the area of Izzy's borrowed Frisbee in inches? _____

6. Competition Frisbees usually have a diameter of 8–10 inches. Which of the Frisbees shown could be used in competition? _____

7. Sacha's Frisbee has a radius of 76.2 millimeters. Which one is it? _____

8. Alice is not Izzy's cousin. Which Frisbee belongs to Alice? _____

Finish Line

Use the information in the box and the chart to answer the questions below.

The track-and-field teams from the United States, Australia, Germany, and Zimbabwe competed against each other in a relay race. The runners from the U.S. took the least time in the first half of the race but longer than Germany's runners in the second half. Australia's team came in behind Zimbabwe's team in the first half of the race but was fastest in the second half. Germany had the slowest time in the first half of the race but took second place in the second half. Zimbabwe had the slowest time in the second half of the relay.

First Half	Second Half
55.29 seconds	40.402 seconds
55.037 seconds	41.2 seconds
55.3 seconds	40.38 seconds
55.295 seconds	40.4 seconds

1. What was each team's total time?

U.S.: _____

Australia: _____

Germany: _____

Zimbabwe: _____

2. What color medal did each team receive?

U.S.: _____

Australia: _____

Germany: _____

Zimbabwe: _____

What a Ride!

Colin is starting a paper route to save up for a new bike. He will be folding and delivering 30 newspapers every morning. On Sundays, he gets a $.25 bonus per paper because the papers are much larger. Use this information to help Colin make decisions about his new job.

1. Colin gets his first check for $105.50. He works the same number of hours every day. How many hours did he work this week? _____

2. Each day, it takes Colin 1 hour and 10 minutes to deliver the papers after he folds them. How many hours per week does he spend folding the papers? _____

3. How many minutes does it take to deliver each paper on average? Express your answer as a decimal. _____

4. The bike Colin wants costs $530. If he gets a 15% student discount before tax, and the tax rate is 7.5%, what would be the total cost of the bike? _____

5. Colin earns the same amount of money each week. If Colin puts 25% of his earnings into a savings account and uses the rest for the bike, how many weeks would he have to work to earn enough to buy the bike? _____

6. Colin is offered another job washing dishes for $7.35 an hour, 12 hours per week. Should he quit his job delivering papers and take the dishwashing job? Explain your reasoning.

_____

_____

Groundhog Day

Every Groundhog Day, eight groundhogs come out of their holes in Shadow Springs and look for their shadows. This year, the sun was shining and all eight of them saw their shadows. All the shadows are in proportion to each other. Based on the measurements of the first groundhog and his shadow, determine the length or height of the others.

1.

?

6"

$$\text{18 in.}$$

2.

21 in

?

_____

3.

54 cm

?

_____

4.

?

8 in

_____

5.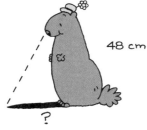

48 cm

?

_____

6.

?

14 cm

_____

7.

?

9 in

_____

8.

60 cm

?

_____

High Score

Ben wants to beat the high score on the Extreme Moon Racer video game. The score he needs is 10,100 points. Ben already has 8,300 points. You earn points in three ways: zero gravity jumping, moon rock climbing, and flag planting. They are scored as shown in the box. Use the information provided to answer the questions below.

EXTREME MOON RACER SCORING GUIDE

Zero gravity jumping: 10 points

Moon rock climbing: 25 points

Flag planting: 100 points

1. How many more points does Ben need to reach the high score? _____

2. If Ben scores the same number of points performing each of the three tasks, how many times does he need to do each task to beat the high score? Show your work.

_____

_____

_____

3. Ben earns 400 points doing flag plants. If he earns twice as many points moon rock climbing as he does zero gravity jumping, how many times does he have to perform each task to beat the high score? Show your work.

_____

_____

_____

4. Ben did 50 zero gravity jumps and 50 moon rock climbs. Did he beat the high score? _____

Framed!

Steve is a new employee in a frame shop. His job is to fit glass panes inside picture frames.
The glass must be $1\frac{1}{4}$ inches smaller on each side to fit inside its frame. Steve needs to know
how much glass to order. Given the following dimensions of frames, give the area of
the glass panes that will fit. Give your answers in decimal form rounded to the nearest hundredth.

1. 3.85×9.125 _____

2. $4\frac{3}{8} \times 6\frac{9}{16}$ _____

3. $5\frac{16}{32} \times 8\frac{8}{16}$ _____

4. 12.625×16.95 _____

A customer has just picked up some framed pictures. She asks for the diagonal measures of the frames.
Help Steve find the length of the diagonal for the following dimensions.

5. 51×68 _____

6. 17.5×42 _____

7. 30.4×57 _____

8. $3\frac{1}{2} \times 12$ _____

A custom frame has been ordered. It will be square and have an opening that is centered
and 25 percent of the size of the whole frame.

9. If the frame must be constructed from four identical pieces of wood that are not
parallelograms, what geometric shape will they be? _____

10. The dimensions of the outside of the frame are 20×20. What are the dimensions of the
opening in the frame? _____

Around the Neighborhood

Read the questions and help the neighbors solve these problems about their daily lives.

1. Three kinds of cake are left over from Lauren's party. Of the coconut cake, $\frac{7}{16}$ was left over. Of the chocolate cake, $37\frac{1}{2}$% was left over. Of the vanilla cake, 0.1875 was left over. If each cake was the same size and had been cut into 32 equal pieces, how many pieces of cake were left?

   a. 16

   b. 32

   c. 24

   d. 8

2. Carolyn is half as tall as Rory. Rory is 35% taller than Enzo. If Enzo is 120 cm tall, how tall is Carolyn?

   a. 155 cm

   b. 185 cm

   c. 162 cm

   d. 81 cm

3. Molly is buying a new rug. She measures the room, and it is 10.3 meters by 12.5 meters. She wants the rug to cover most of the floor but not touch any of the walls. Which rug has the best dimensions for her room?

   a. 90 cm × 130 cm

   b. 90 m × 130 m

   c. 9,000 cm × 11,000 cm

   d. 900 cm × 1,100 cm

4. Adriane forgot some of the ingredients for the cake she is baking. She went to the store with a 10-dollar bill and bought baking soda for $1.29, $1\frac{1}{3}$ pounds of bananas costing $0.39 per pound, chocolate chips for $2.88, and two boxes of sugar for $.79 each. She also had a coupon for the chocolate chips for $.40 off. How much change did she get?

   a. $3.09

   b. $4.13

   c. $3.73

   d. $4.25

5. Missy takes her Yorkie, Birdie, to the dog run. She notices that the dogs belong to only 3 breeds, and that there are fewer than 20 dogs there. If there are 4 times as many poodles as there are Maltese, and 3 times as many Yorkies as there are Maltese, how many Maltese are there?

   a. 2

   b. 4

   c. 6

   d. 8

6. John's batting averages for the 5 seasons he's been playing have been as follows: 0.135, 0.220, 0.198, 0.236, 0.241. What is his lifetime average?

   a. 0.166

   b. 0.206

   c. 0.204

   d. 0.220

7. Andrea purchases 2 dresses They retail for $35.50 and $28.80. The store is offering a special: if you buy 2 dresses, the less expensive dress is 20% off. The tax rate is 6%. How much does Andrea spend on the 2 dresses?

   a. $88.90

   b. $94.23

   c. $52.77

   d. $62.05

8. Adam is buying gas for his scooter. He uses .57 gallons daily for his 40-mile round-trip commute to work. If he works Monday–Friday, and gas costs $3.71 per gallon, what is his weekly gas cost per mile commuted?

   a. $.26

   b. $.05

   c. $.61

   d. $.57

Flip-Flopping

Use the graph to answer the questions below.

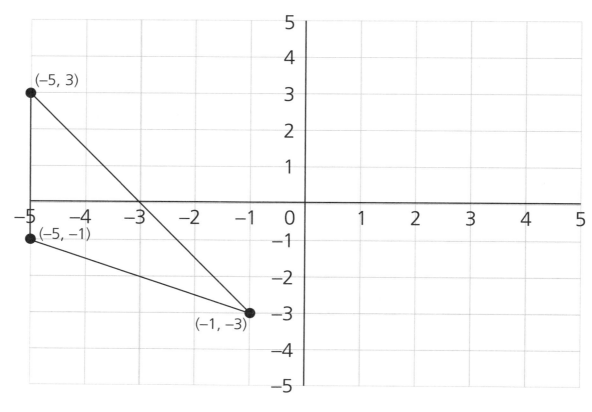

1. Draw a reflection of this figure on the graph.

2. Name the corresponding points between the two figures.

(−5, −1) corresponds to _____

(−5, 3) corresponds to _____

(−1, −3) corresponds to _____

3. Draw rotation of this figure.

4. Name the corresponding points between the two figures.

(−5, −1) corresponds to _____

(−5, 3) corresponds to _____

(−1, −3) corresponds to _____

5. Draw a translation of this figure.

6. Name the corresponding points between the two figures.

(−5, −1) corresponds to _____

(−5, 3) corresponds to _____

(−1, −3) corresponds to _____

Mall Mayhem

Use the information provided to answer the following questions about a day at the mall.

1. Marina went back-to-school shopping at the mall. She bought 6 tops and 4 pairs of pants to mix and match. How many combinations can she make? Show your work. _____

_____

2. Marina's friend Lydia bought 4 tops and 5 pairs of pants. How many combinations can she make? Show your work. _____

_____

3. Shoes at Marty's Shoe Shack are on sale. Boots are 2 pairs for $36. Sneakers are $23. Dress shoes are $28. If you buy any 3 pairs, you get 20% off your total purchase. April bought 1 pair of dress shoes and 2 pairs of boots. If she spent $88, how many pairs of sneakers did she buy? _____

4. Jasper's Juice Bar sells 7 kinds of fruit juice and 3 kinds of vegetable juice. Christopher wants a drink made from 2 kinds of fruit juice and 1 kind of vegetable juice. How many choices does he have? Show your work. _____

_____

5. Oscar wants a drink made of 3 kinds of fruit juice. How many choices does he have? Show your work. _____

_____

6. Blake buys tokens at the Penny Arcade. Tokens are 3 for $1 or 20 for $5. Blake gets 49 tokens. What is the least amount of money he could have spent on them? _____

Angle Art

Draw the angles described below. Use a protractor to be certain your angles are correct.

1. A pair of complementary angles. One angle is 63°.

2. A pair of supplementary angles. One angle is 101°.

3. A pair of adjacent angles. One is 59°. One is 33°.

4. A pair of adjacent angles. Both angles are right angles.

5. A pair of complementary angles. One angle is 10°.

6. A pair of supplementary angles. One angle is 10°.

Turn Up the Volume

Answer the questions below.

1. A cube has a length of 1 inch, a width of 1 inch, and a height of 1 inch. What is its volume? _____

2. Draw the figure described in question 1.

3. Chester is building a prism made of blocks. Each block is 1 cubic inch (1 inch × 1 inch × 1 inch). If he creates a prism that is 7 inches long, 4 inches wide, and 1 inch high, what is its volume? _____

4. Draw the figure described in question 3.

5. Chester adds 2 more layers of blocks to his prism, making the height 3 inches. What is its volume? _____

6. Draw the figure described in question 5.

7. Chester takes down his first prism and builds a new one with the same 1-inch cubes. The new structure has a length of 4 inches, a width of 3 inches, and a height of 7 inches. What is its volume? _____

8. Draw the structure described in question 7.

An Exercise in Size

Choose the best answer for the following questions about size.

1. Who is taller?

    a. a person who is 4 feet 10 inches

    b. a person who is 152 centimeters

2. Which animal weighs more?

    a. an African elephant that weighs 14,000 pounds

    b. a gray whale that weighs 36 tons

3. Which is taller?

    a. an ostrich that is 96 inches

    b. an emu that is 5 feet

4. If 2 gallons of pink lemonade cost the same as 6 quarts of pink lemonade, which is a better value? _____

5. If 5 pints of milk cost the same as a half gallon of milk, which is cheaper?

_____

6. A recipe calls for 4 cups of sugar. You have a package of sugar labeled 2 pints. Do you have enough sugar for the recipe? _____

7. Which is smaller?

    a. a ladybug that is 0.4 inches

    b. a housefly that is 8 millimeters

8. Which is taller?

    a. a camel that is 2 meters

    b. a moose that is 6 feet

Start Your Engines!

Use the chart to answer the questions below.

ACE PUTTY'S STOCK CAR CUP RESULTS FOR JUNE

Race	Distance (miles)	Time (hours)
1	600	4.54
2	400	3.10
3	500	3.16

1. How many races were there in June? _____

2. In which race did Ace Putty have the fastest average speed? _____

3. What was the total distance Ace raced in June? _____

4. What was Ace's average speed for all 3 races combined? Round up to the nearest whole number.

_____

5. Ace finished the 400-mile race in 3.01 hours last year. What was his average speed in that race? Round up to the nearest whole number. _____

6. The winner of Race 1 had an average speed of 137 miles per hour. What was his time? _____

7. The winner of Race 2 had an average speed of 139 miles per hour. What was her time? _____

8. The winner of Race 3 had an average speed of 158 miles per hour. Who won the race? _____

The Daily Grind

Answer the following questions about Paul's daily activities.

1. On Monday, Paul vacuumed the whole house. He discovered a huge amount of change in the couch cushions. He had a total of 70 dimes and quarters. If the value of the dimes was equal to the value of the quarters, how many of each coin did he have? _____

2. On Tuesday, Paul went to a baseball game. In the first inning, the Eagles hit a grand slam. The Eagles scored 2 runs in each even-numbered inning, and scored an additional 2 runs in each inning that is a perfect square. In each prime-numbered inning, the Hornets scored a number of runs equal to the inning number. No other runs were scored. Which team won the game? What was the score? _____

_____

3. On Wednesday, Paul did his laundry. He realized he was out of liquid detergent, and he bought more. He discovered that the detergent he usually buys in a 100-fluid-ounce container is now concentrated to double strength. How many fewer pounds will the container weigh if one cup of detergent weighs 0.52 pounds? _____

On Saturday, Paul paid his bills. Of the total amount he paid, 50% went to his mortgage payment, 25% went to his car payment, 20% went to his utility bills, and the remaining $70 went to his phone bill. How much did he pay for each of the other bills?

4. Mortgage _____

5. Car payment _____

6. Utilities _____

BricKload

Bruce Strong is a passionate brick collector. He has big bricks, small bricks, and bricks of all different colors. Bruce's friend, Tiny, found a shiny green and fuchsia brick for Bruce's collection. Tiny needs to choose the best box in which to carry Bruce's brick. Use your knowledge of volume and the information given to answer the questions below.

> Bruce's new brick has a length of 12 inches, a width of 3 inches, and a height of 2 inches.

1. What is the volume of Bruce's new brick? _____

2. Draw a diagram of the brick.

3. What is the volume of the brick in cubic centimeters? Round your answer to the nearest whole number. _____

Tiny's Boxes

BOX A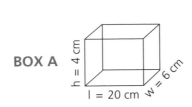

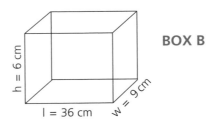 BOX B

4. What is the volume of Box A? _____

5. What is the volume of Box B? _____

6. Which of the boxes would be the best fit for the brick? _____

Slide Over!

For each point on the top rectangle, write its corresponding point on its translation.

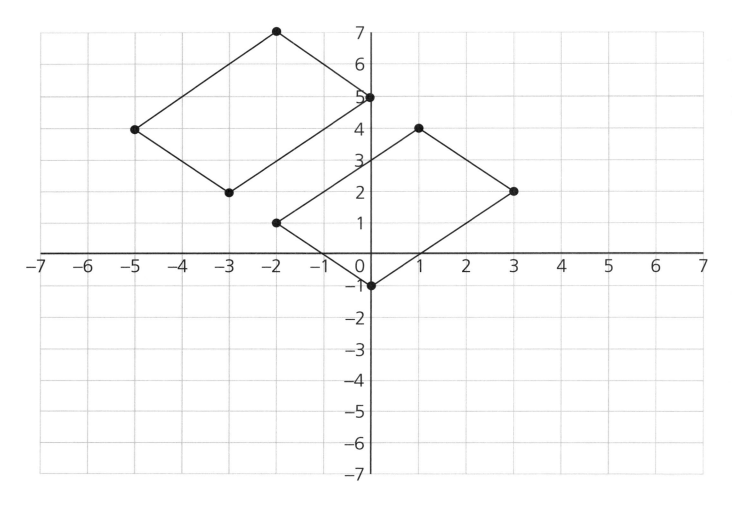

1. _____ corresponds to _____.

2. _____ corresponds to _____.

3. _____ corresponds to _____.

4. _____ corresponds to _____.

5. Create a second polygon anywhere on the graph.

6. Draw a translation of your new shape.

Time Twister

Calculate the time described in each question below.

1. 257 minutes after 3:00 PM   _____

2. 73 minutes before noon   _____

3. 99 minutes before 1:30 AM   _____

4. 514 minutes before midnight   _____

5. 270 minutes before 5:15 AM   _____

6. 57 minutes after the answer to question 5   _____

7. 4,080 seconds after 3:10 PM   _____

8. 770 minutes after 4:11 AM   _____

9. 100 minutes, 960 seconds before 8:16 PM   _____

10. 23^2 minutes before 9:25 PM   _____

Areas of Africa

Use the information provided to answer the questions below.

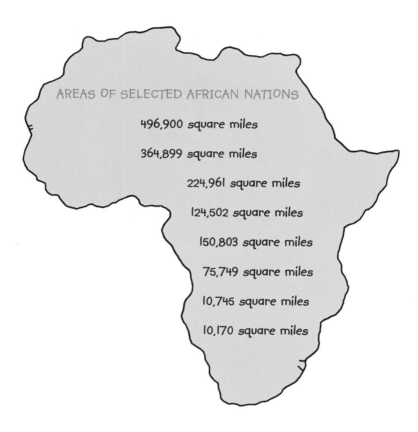

AREAS OF SELECTED AFRICAN NATIONS

496,900 square miles

364,899 square miles

224,961 square miles

124,502 square miles

150,803 square miles

75,749 square miles

10,745 square miles

10,170 square miles

1. The continent of Africa has an area of 11,700,000 square miles. Sudan has an area of 967,493 square miles. What percentage of Africa does Sudan cover? Round to the nearest whole number. _____

2. The Democratic Republic of the Congo is 905,563 square miles. Brazzaville is 132,046 square miles. What percentage of the Democratic Republic of the Congo would Brazzaville fill? Round to the nearest whole number. _____

3. Kenya's area and the Ivory Coast's area differ by about 100,000 square miles. Kenya is larger. The areas of both countries are included in the chart above. What is Kenya's area?

_____

4. Based on what you learned in question 3, what is Ivory Coast's area? _____

5. Rwanda and Burundi have nearly the same area. The areas of both countries are included in the chart above. Rwanda is the smaller country. What is its area? _____

Pasture Pastime

To answer the barnyard riddle in the box, solve the problems below to determine the value of n. Using the key at the bottom of the page, find the letter that matches your numeric answer. Mark that letter in the square to the right of each question. Read from top to bottom to answer the riddle!

Where did Farmer Pete's prize Cow eat popcorn?

1. $n^2 - 9^3 = -629$ _____ ☐

2. $1.8 \times 3.9 + 0.98 = n$ _____ ☐

3. $\dfrac{7}{2} + \dfrac{10}{4} + \dfrac{22}{11} = n$ _____ ☐

4. $n^2 + 8^2 = 388$ _____ ☐

5. $27 - 6n = -15$ _____ ☐

6. $5\,(0.35n + 1.25) = 13.25$ _____ ☐

7. $19n - 75 = -18$ _____ ☐

8. $\dfrac{18}{3} \div \dfrac{10}{5} = n$ _____ ☐

9. $20.20 \div n = 4.04$ _____ ☐

10. $\dfrac{3}{4} \times \dfrac{n}{9} = 1$ _____ ☐

11. $133 - 18n = 7$ _____ ☐

12. $7^3 - 350 = 2n$ _____ ☐

Key
−3.5 = S
3 = O
4 = M
5 = V
7 = E
8 = T
10 = A
12 = I
18 = H

Olympic Greatness

Michael Johnson, a track and field athlete, set 2 individual Olympic world records in the 1996 Atlanta games. Solve the following problems to learn more about American Olympic Games history! (Note: when an Olympic time is given, 3:22.56, for example, it means 3 minutes, 22 seconds, 56 hundredths of a second.)

1. Michael Johnson's winning time in the 200-meter sprint was 19.32. How many meters per second did he run? _____

2. In his second record-setting race, his time was 43.49, and he ran an average of 9.197 meters per second. How many meters long was the race? _____

3. Johnson was also part of a record-setting 4 × 400 relay in the Barcelona games of 1992. If the total time for the team was 2:55.74, how many meters per second did each team member average? _____

4. In the Seoul games of 1988, Florence Griffith Joyner won the 200-meter sprint. Her time was 21.34. How much faster was Johnson's winning 200-meter time in Atlanta than Joyner's in Seoul, expressed as a percentage? _____

5. Joyner's sister-in-law, Jackie Joyner-Kersee, also set a world record in the Seoul games, in the heptathlon. Her total score was 7,291. She scored 1,172 on hurdles; 1,054 on high jump; 915 on shot put; 1,264 on long jump; 776 on javelin; and 987 on the 800-meter run. What was her score on the 200-meter run? _____

6. In her record-breaking race at the 2000 games in Sydney, Brooke Bennett swam an average of 0.624 meters per second in the 800-meter freestyle. What was her time in minutes and seconds (rounded to the nearest second)? _____

7. Shannon Miller has won the most medals of any American gymnast in history. She has won 16 medals in major world championships. If 0.56 of her medals are from other competitions, how many Olympic medals has she won? _____

Use the chart to solve the problems below.

ALL-TIME TRACK & FIELD MEDALS, 1896–2004

Rank	Nation	Gold	Silver	Bronze	Total
1	USA	304		182	715
2	Soviet Union		55	74	193
3	Great Britain	48	76		184
4	Finland		35	29	112
5	East Germany	38		35	109

8. Determine the missing figures for each country and write them into the chart.

9. Which country has won the highest proportion of gold medals relative to total medals?

_____

10. Which country's ratio of gold:silver:bronze is 12:19:15? _____

Triangle Tangle

Identify which type of triangle (*acute*, *right*, or *obtuse*) would have the following angles.

1. 70°, 60°, 50° _____

2. 80°, 50°, 50° _____

3. 90°, 45°, 45° _____

4. 110°, 40°, 30° _____

5. 97°, 60°, 23° _____

6. 90°, 65°, 25° _____

Identify which type of triangle (*equilateral*, *isosceles*, or *scalene*) would have the following sides.

7. 9 inches, 4.5 inches, 9 inches _____

8. 5 centimeters, 2 centimeters, 4 centimeters _____

9. 3 feet, 3 feet, 3 feet _____

Determine the missing angle for each.

10. 100°, 50° _____

11. 90°, 18° _____

12. 88°, 41° _____

Batting-Cage Battle

Jake and 3 friends spend an hour at the batting cages. They each hit 10 balls. The chart represents the speeds at which they hit the ball. Use the information in the chart to answer the questions below.

Jake	Travis	Mark	Drew
83.2 mph	68.5 mph	67.4 mph	80.7 mph
79.8 mph	70.3 mph	69.3 mph	82.3 mph
80.1 mph	72.5 mph	65.0 mph	83.4 mph
88.5 mph	69.0 mph	70.2 mph	86.5 mph
85.2 mph	72.3 mph	66.8 mph	79.8 mph
83.8 mph	66.5 mph	59.9 mph	77.9 mph
88.1 mph	71.3 mph	63.6 mph	81.6 mph
87.9 mph	74.8 mph	58.0 mph	83.5 mph
90.0 mph	70.9 mph	70.1 mph	86.0 mph
85.3 mph	69.1 mph	68.4 mph	81.0 mph

1. What is Travis's mean batting speed? _____

2. Who has the largest range of batting speeds? _____

3. What is Mark's median batting speed? _____

4. The next day, Drew returned to the batting cages, but he used a different bat. His batting speed improved by 8.3% overall. What was his new mean speed? _____

5. If at 1 mph the ball travels at 1.47 feet per second, how many feet will the ball travel in 1.5 seconds at Travis's best batting speed? _____

6. Due to several factors, a pitched ball slows down about 1 mph every 7 feet as it approaches the plate. If a ball is pitched at 90 mph and the distance from the mound to the plate is 60 feet, at what speed is the ball traveling when it reaches the plate? _____

Gone to the Dogs

To answer the canine conundrum in the box, solve the problems below to determine the value of *n*. Using the key at the bottom of the page, find the letter that matches your numeric answer. Mark that letter in the square to the right of each question. Read from top to bottom to answer the riddle!

1. 15% of 80 = *n* _____ ☐

2. $n^2 + 17 = 42$ _____ ☐

3. $82 - 19n = 25$ _____ ☐

4. $n^2 - 9^2 = 19$ _____ ☐

5. $\frac{15}{2} \times \frac{2}{n} = 3$ _____ ☐

6. $(10^3 + 2(50 + 50)) \div n = 200$ _____ ☐

7. $9\frac{1}{3} \div \frac{2}{3} = n$ _____ ☐

8. $n^3 - 3 = 24$ _____ ☐

9. $n \times 0.16 = 13.6$ _____ ☐

10. $19 - 2n = 7$ _____ ☐

11. $-4^3 \times \frac{1}{n} = -4$ _____ ☐

12. $2(n + 6) = 38$ _____ ☐

3 = E

5 = H

6 = A

10 = Y

12 = T

13 = K

14 = V

16 = R

85 = B

Around the World

Use the information in the box to solve the problems below.

Charlotte, Darby, Grace, Bevin, and Emma are international pen pals. Each girl lives in a different city with varying weather. One girl lives in Kiev, one girl lives in Boston, one girl lives in Dublin, one girl lives in Chicago, and one girl lives in Shanghai. Grace and Bevin both live in capital cities. Darby lives in the city with the highest temperature.

Charlotte is from Boston, where the temperature is 30°C. The temperature in degrees Celsius in Shanghai is 10 degrees warmer than the temperature in Dublin. The temperature in degrees Fahrenheit in Kiev is 5 degrees warmer than the temperature in Boston. The temperature in Dublin in degrees Celsius is 5 degrees cooler than the temperature in Boston. The temperature in degrees Fahrenheit in Chicago is 5 degrees cooler than the temperature in Dublin. Darby and Grace both live outside of the United States.

Where does each girl live?

1. Emma lives in _____.

2. Charlotte lives in _____.

3. Darby lives in _____.

4. Grace lives in _____.

5. Bevin lives in _____.

In degrees Fahrenheit, what is the temperature of each city?

6. It is _____ in Dublin.

7. It is _____ in Boston.

8. It is _____ in Chicago.

9. It is _____ in Kiev.

10. It is _____ in Shanghai.

Lemonade Stand

Use the information provided to answer the questions below.

1. Laila and Leanne decided to run a lemonade stand in their neighborhood. They started by mixing 17 gallons of lemonade. How many quarts did they mix? _____

2. One container of lemonade mix makes 20 quarts of lemonade. How many containers of lemonade mix do they need? _____

3. To make the lemonade, you need 2 teaspoons of lemonade mix per cup. How many teaspoons of lemonade mix are needed to make $3\frac{1}{2}$ cups? _____

4. The friends could also make the lemonade by combining $\frac{3}{4}$ scoop of lemonade mix with 1 quart of water. How many scoops would they need to make a gallon of lemonade? _____

5. Laila pours 1 cup of lemonade into each glass. How many glasses of lemonade will 17 gallons make? _____

6. Plastic glasses cost $3.99 for 100. How much money did they spend on glasses? _____

7. Laila and Leanne sell all 17 gallons of lemonade! They charged $0.50 per glass. Leanne's father gave them $5 for one glass because he said it was the best lemonade he ever had. Laila gave 1 girl a free glass of lemonade because she had no money with her. How much money did the girls make? _____

8. The lemonade mix cost $4.65 per container, and each container makes 20 quarts of lemonade. How much money did the girls spend on mix to make the 17 gallons of lemonade? _____

9. Was Laila and Leanne's lemonade stand profitable? Explain. _____

_____

_____

10. If Laila and Leanne increased the cost of their lemonade by 25%, what would their profit have been after they covered their expenses? _____

11. Laila and Leanne decide to expand their drink stand to include iced tea. They mix up 12 gallons of iced tea. How many quarts do they mix? _____

12. If Leanne pours 1 cup of iced tea into each glass, how many glasses of iced tea will 12 gallons make? _____

Tumbling Down

Allen is posting sequences on the bulletin board. He has been asked to also post the next number in each sequence. Help Allen select the correct equation to figure out the next number in each set.

1. 3, 10, 31, 94

   a. $3(x + 1)$

   b. $3x + 1$

   c. $(x - 1)\,3$

   d. $3(x - 1)$

2. 100, 46, 19, 5.5

   a. $x \div (2 - 4)$

   b. $\frac{x}{2} - 4$

   c. $\frac{x-4}{2}$

   d. $2x - 4$

3. −12, −1, 4.5, 7.25

   a. $\frac{x+2}{10}$

   b. $2x + 10$

   c. $\frac{x}{2} - 10$

   d. $\frac{x+10}{2}$

4. $\frac{1}{4}$, 5, 100, 2000

   a. $10\left(\frac{x}{\frac{1}{2}}\right)$

   b. $\frac{10x}{2}$

   c. $10x\left(\frac{1}{2}\right)$

   d. $\frac{1}{2}(10x)$

5. 3, 7, 47, 2207

   a. $\frac{x}{2} - 2$

   b. $\frac{x^2}{2}$

   c. $\sqrt{x-2}$

   d. $x^2 - 2$

6. 12, −22, 12, −22

   a. $\frac{x-10}{-1}$

   b. $\frac{10x}{-1}$

   c. $\frac{x}{-1} - 10$

   d. $x - 10$

Now complete the tables to show possible solutions for the equations.

7. $x + 5 = y$

x	y	(x, y)
−3	2	(−3, 2)
−1		
0		
1		
2		
3		

8. $3x = y$

x	y	(x, y)
−5	−15	(−5, −15)
−3		
−1		
0		
2		
5		

Youngtown Years

Use the pie chart to answer the questions below.

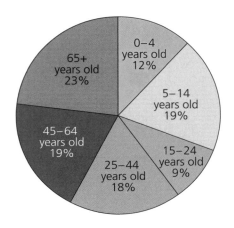

1. What is the largest age group in Youngstown? _____

2. What is the smallest age group in Youngstown? _____

3. Youngstown has a population of 17,800. How many people are 65 or older? _____

4. How many people are less than 5 years old? _____

5. Youngstown plans to expand its high school over the next 5 years. What is one reason they might be planning the expansion? _____

6. 356 people in Youngstown are 90 or older. What percentage of the population is over 90 years of age? _____

7. A new factory opens and 712 people move to Youngstown. By what percentage has the town's population grown? _____

8. Describe how you could present the information in this pie chart as a bar graph.

_____

_____

_____

_____

Formula Racing

Find a stopwatch or a clock with a second hand. Read the questions, and provide the formulas requested below. Use the timer to see how long it takes you to answer all of the questions.

1. Area of a circle

_____

2. Diameter of a circle

_____

3. Area of a right triangle

_____

4. Area of a square

_____

5. Volume of a rectangular prism

_____

6. Perimeter of a rectangle

_____

7. Area of a rectangle

_____

8. Area of an equilateral triangle

_____

9. Circumference of a circle

_____

10. Volume of a pyramid/triangular prism

_____

11. Area of a parallelogram

_____

12. Volume of a cylinder

_____

Your Time _____

Taking Stock

Use the information in the box to answer the questions below.

U.S. STOCK MARKETS: SEPTEMBER 16
NASDAQ 2310.96
−14.59 ▼ −0.63%
DJIA 11326.32
−51.7 ▼ −0.45%
S&P 1260.31
−7.07 ▼ −0.56%

1. What was the NASDAQ's value when the markets closed on September 15? _____

2. What number did the DJIA (Dow Jones Industrial Average) reach by the close of business on September 15? _____

3. The S&P 500's value rose by 5.27 on September 17. What was the percentage change? Round your answer to the nearest hundredth of a percent. _____

4. The NASDAQ rose by 51.54 points on September 17. What was the percentage change? Round your answer to the nearest hundredth of a percent. _____

5. The DJIA rose by 1.10% on September 17. How many points does this represent? Round your answer to the nearest hundredth. _____

6. In the last 52 weeks, the DJIA has reached a high of 14,280. What is the difference in points between September 16 and the DJIA's 52-week high? _____

7. What is the percentage difference between September 16 and the DJIA's 52-week high? Round your answer to the nearest whole number. _____

8. What is the percentage difference between September 16 and the DJIA's 52-week low of 10,732? Round your answer to the nearest whole number. _____

Brain Games

Challenge your brain with these mind-bending math games!

1. How can you move just 3 of these pennies to flip this triangle upside down? Draw arrows on the image to show how you'd do it.

2. How can you move just 2 of these toothpicks in order to create 7 squares? Draw in the placement of your toothpicks to show how you'd do it.

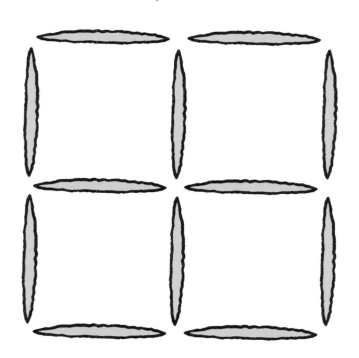

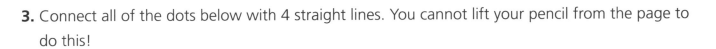

3. Connect all of the dots below with 4 straight lines. You cannot lift your pencil from the page to do this!

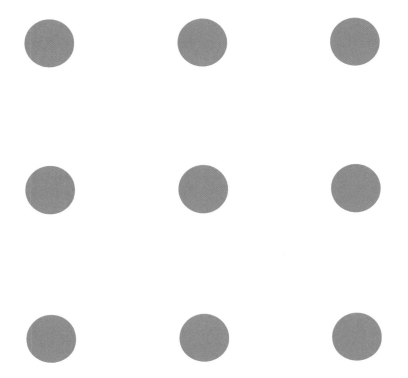

4. You have to plant 10 oak tree saplings in 5 rows with 4 trees in each row. How can you do it? Draw your tree pattern below.

Pattern Play

Use the sets of numbers below to solve the problems. First, find the square of the middle number in the set. Then, multiply the first and last numbers of the set, and add 1 to their product. Use the example in the box as a guide.

> Example:
>
> 2, 3, 4 $3^2 = 9$ $(2 \times 4) + 1 = 8 + 1 = 9$

1. 3, 4, 5   _____   _____

2. 45, 46, 47   _____   _____

3. 99, 100, 101   _____   _____

4. What pattern do you see in your calculations? _____

_____

5. Draw the next figure to complete the pattern. Then, write 2 rules that describe the pattern.

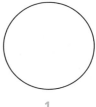 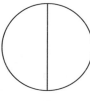 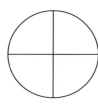 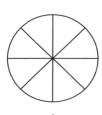

    1   2   3   4   5

_____

_____

6. Draw the next figure to complete the pattern. Then, write 2 rules that describe the pattern.

    1   2   3   4

_____

_____

Graphing Inequalities

Write the inequality shown in each number line.

1.

_____

2.

_____

3.

_____

4.

_____

Draw a line showing the solution for each inequality.
Don't forget to leave the circle open to show **<** or **>**, and to fill in the circle for **≤** or **≥**.

5. $x \geq -3$

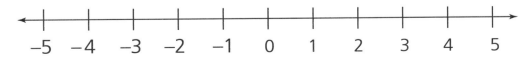

6. $x < 5$

Animal Farm

Write the coordinates of each animal found on the graph.

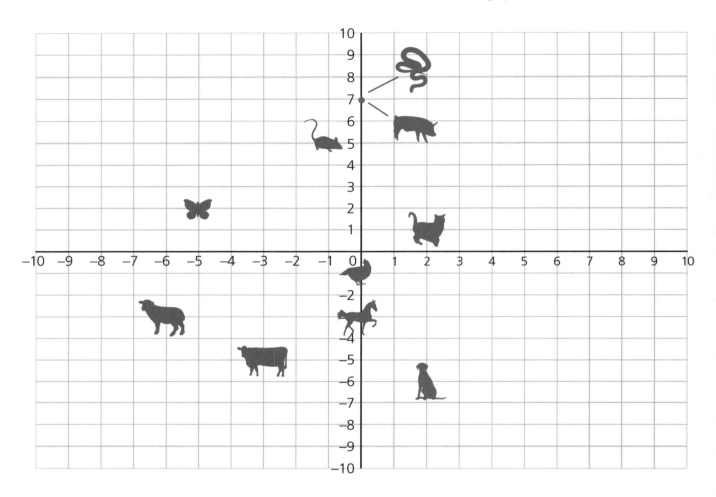

1. Pig   _____

2. Mouse   _____

3. Butterfly   _____

4. Cat   _____

5. Snake   _____

6. Horse   _____

7. Dog   _____

8. Cow   _____

9. Chicken   _____

10. Sheep   _____

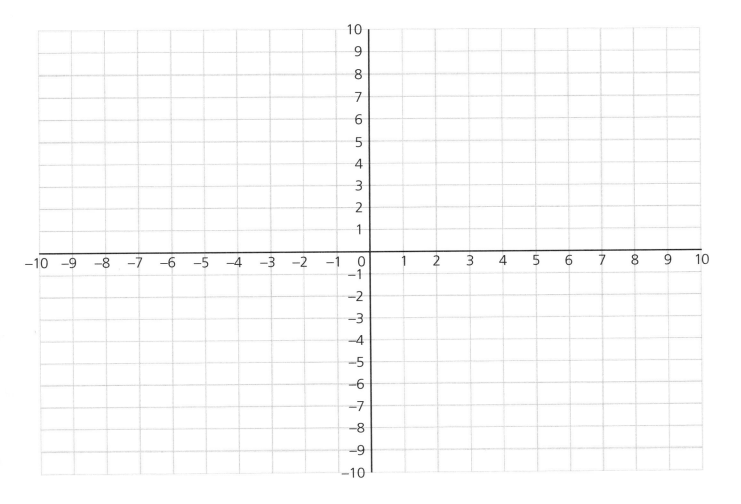

11. The barn is at (0, 0). Draw it on the graph.

12. The farmer's house is at (0, –8). Draw it on the graph.

13. The water well is at (5, –3). Draw it on the graph.

14. The pig's trough is at (1, 7). Draw it on the graph.

15. The stable is at (4, 1). Draw it on the graph.

16. The chicken coop is at (–3, –2). Draw it on the graph.

Nothing but Net!

A basketball player's free-throw percentage is calculated by dividing the number of free-throw shots made by the number of free-throw shots taken. Calculate each player's free-throw percentage below. Round your answer to the nearest whole number.

1. Player 1   Shots made: 85   Shots taken: 107   _____

2. Player 2   Shots made: 92   Shots taken: 115   _____

3. Player 3   Shots made: 89   Shots taken: 98   _____

4. Player 4   Shots made: 12   Shots taken: 18   _____

5. Player 5   Shots made: 48   Shots taken: 75   _____

6. Player 6   Shots made: 63   Shots taken: 91   _____

7. Player 7   Shots made: 58   Shots taken: 70   _____

8. Player 8   Shots made: 87   Shots taken: 118   _____

9. Player 9   Shots made: 91   Shots taken: 111   _____

10. Player 10   Shots made: 54   Shots taken: 68   _____

11. Player 11   Shots made: 64   Shots taken: 70   _____

12. Player 12   Shots made: 87   Shots taken: 93   _____

Use the free-throw percentages that you calculated to answer the following questions. Round your answers to the nearest whole number.

13. Use the team's free-throw percentages to create a pie chart. Group the free throws into the following categories: <65%; 65–75%; 76%–85%; 86%–95%; >95%.

14. What is this team's average free-throw percentage? _____

15. What is the median free-throw percentage? _____

16. What is the mode free-throw percentage? _____

17. What is the range for free-throw percentages? _____

18. If you were on the opposing team and could foul either Player 6 or Player 9, forcing him or her to shoot, who would you choose? _____

19. If Player 1 makes 15 of her next 19 free-throw shots, what will her new free-throw percentage be? _____

20. If Player 4 makes 15 of his next 19 shots, what will his new free-throw percentage be? _____

Equation Quest

Express each of the following statements as an equation. Use *n* as your variable. Solve each equation for *n*.

1. There are 6 bats hanging from a porch roof and $\frac{1}{3}$ of the total number of bats in a nearby tree. How many bats are there in total? _____

2. Sadiq is driving 40 miles per hour in his car. Sadiq's friend Thane is driving another car. Sadiq and Thane's average speed is 48 miles per hour. How fast is Thane driving? _____

3. Mr. Maxwell assigned the following English homework this week:

Read 23 pages of the novel on Monday.
Read 27 pages of the novel on Tuesday.
Read 31 pages of the novel on Wednesday.
Read 22 pages of the novel on Thursday.
Finish the book over the weekend.

If the novel is 144 pages long, how many pages must be read over the weekend? _____

4. Jo Idaho is playing 5 concerts at the civic center. The venue has 28,342 seats. A total of 2,588 seats were given away for promotional purposes. How many tickets went on sale for all 5 shows?

_____

5. Clay spent $15.09 at the grocery store. He spent $12.34 at the mall. Dylan paid him back the $5.50 he owed him when they met for lunch. Lunch cost $6.77. Clay came home with $17.90. With how much money did he start out? _____

_____

6. Ana has 4 times as many markers as Adelaide. Adelaide has half as many markers as Miles. George has 7 markers. There are 56 markers. How many does each person have?

_____

_____

7. Gwen baked 3 dozen cookies. Lori ate $\frac{1}{9}$ of them. Dad ate 3 more. How many cookies are left?

_____

8. Grandma made 2 sweaters for Trish, 1 sweater for Robert, 2 sweaters for Craig, and 3 sweaters for Randall. She uses 3 balls of yarn per sweater. Grandma spent a total of $166.80 on yarn. How much does each ball of yarn cost? _____

_____

Three Sides to Every Story

Calculate the perimeter of the following triangles.

1. A scalene triangle with 1 side that measures 9 inches and 2 sides that measure 22 inches combined. _____

2. An isosceles triangle with 2 sides larger than 10 centimeters. One side is 11 centimeters. The other side is 6 centimeters. _____

3. An equilateral triangle with a side that is one-quarter the length of the perimeter in question 2.

_____

4. An isosceles triangle with 1 side measuring 5 centimeters, 1 side measuring 9 centimeters, and a perimeter that is less than 20 centimeters. _____

5. A scalene triangle with a height of 6 inches and an area of 9 square inches. One side is 7.5 inches and another side is 9.75 inches. _____

6. How long is each side of the triangle in question 5? _____

7. An equilateral triangle with a side equal to 4^3 inches $-$ 7^2 inches. _____

8. An isosceles triangle has the same perimeter as a six-inch square. _____

Sailing Seth

Sailing Seth is about to set off on a trip to the South Seas. Answer the following tricky problems about his voyage.

1. Sailing Seth is bringing a family photo along with him to remember everyone he loves. In the photos, Sailing Seth sees: 1 grandfather, 1 grandmother, 2 fathers, 2 mothers, 6 children, 4 grandchildren, 2 sisters, 2 brothers, 3 sons, 3 daughters, 1 father-in-law, 1 mother-in-law, and 1 daughter-in-law. What is the fewest number of people that appear in the family photo? Explain who they are. _____

_____

_____

2. Sailing Seth's nemesis, Evil Erlick, is attempting to beat Sailing Seth to Iguana Island in the South Seas. Both sailors are leaving from Port Peach. The total distance from Port Peach to Iguana Island is 4,300 km. Evil Erlick has a 2-day head start on Sailing Seth. Evil Erlick is traveling at a rate of 60 kilometers per day. Sailing Seth wants to arrive on Iguana Island 5 days before Evil Erlick. How fast must Sailing Seth travel to do this? Round your answer to the nearest whole number.

Hit the Slopes

Noah, Mary, Andy, Mia, Alex, and Alison are headed from New York City to Vermont for a week of skiing. Use the chart to answer the following questions about their trip.

Person	Transportation	Cost Per Person	Travel Time	Notes
Noah	own car	$42	6.5 hours	shared cost with Mary
Mary	own car	$42	6.5 hours	
Andy	rental car	$184	8 hours	shared with Alison, hit traffic
Alison	rental car	$184	8 hours	shared with Andy, hit traffic
Mia	plane	$179	3.5 hours	incl. 45-min airport shuttle
Alex	train	$98	9.5 hours	incl. 30-minute taxi

1. Based on the information above, what is the best transportation option if you want to get there quickly? _____

2. What is the slowest way to get to Vermont? _____

3. What is the least expensive way to get to Vermont? _____

All the guests in the ski house share the food and drink costs for the trip equally. Andy brought food worth $13.07, and Alison brought drinks worth $26.95. Later, the others went to the supermarket and spent $128.93.

4. After all the costs were added up, how much additional money did Alison have to put in?

_____

5. After all the costs were added up, how much additional money did Andy have to put in?

_____

6. How much did each person contribute? _____

Mia and Mary go to the lodge to buy lift tickets for the group for Sunday through Wednesday.
Use the fee chart to answer the questions below.

LIFT TICKET PRICES

	1 Day	2 Days	3 Days	4 Days	5 Days
Mon–Fri	$72	$132	$180	$229	$280
Sat–Sun	$77	$144			

7. How much would the total price be per person according to the chart? _____

8. They learn there is a special. Ladies save $20 on a three-day weekday lift ticket. How much would Alison, Mia, and Mary have to pay in total to ski on Sunday, Monday, Tuesday, and Wednesday? _____

9. Noah gets a 15% discount on any tickets he buys for himself for a weekday. What would his total ticket price be? _____

10. Alex will not be skiing on Sunday. What would be the total price for tickets for all 6 skiers?

_____

Dressed to the Nines

Kelly wants to make a new dress for the spring dance. Help her solve the problems below so she can plan out her sewing project.

1. Kelly has found a dress pattern she likes. The pattern requires $2\frac{5}{8}$ yards of fabric. If bolts of fabric have a standard width of 36 inches, how many inches in length should her fabric be?

_____

2. There are several fabrics that Kelly likes. Silk shantung is $10.95 per yard, taffeta is $8.49 per yard, crepe is $9.25 per yard, and silk satin is $9.69 per yard. If Kelly spent $25.43 on $2\frac{5}{8}$ yards of fabric, which fabric did she choose? _____

3. The pattern calls for a 14-inch zipper. The zipper is then covered with fabric that closes with hooks and eyes. If the first hook and eye is to be placed at the top edge and spaced every $1\frac{1}{4}$ inch down the zipper, and there are 4 hooks and eyes per package, how many packages of hooks and eyes will Kelly need to buy? _____

4. Kelly also needs to buy notions for her dress. For the requirements of the pattern, thread is $0.79, a zipper is $1.59, each package of hooks and eyes is $1.19, and interfacing is $1.89. The dress also requires a belt. The 3 belt options are silver for $7.65, striped for $8.25, and gold for $6.50. If her budget is $40, which belt(s) can she afford? Remember that she also has to purchase the fabric mentioned in question #2. _____

5. Kelly must determine what size to make the dress using a size chart that came with the pattern, measured in inches. Unfortunately, her tape measure is metric, and she must measure herself in centimeters. If Kelly's measurements are 86.3 cm bust, 66 cm waist, and 91.4 cm hips, what size should she make the dress according to the chart? _____

SIZING CHART

Size	4	6	8	10
Bust	32	34	36	38
Waist	24	26	28	30
Hips	34	36	38	40

6. The bodice (upper part) of the dress is constructed from 5 pieces of fabric: 1 in front, 2 on the sides, and 2 on the back. When they are sewn together, a certain amount of fabric is left on the inside of the seam. For regular seams, the amount is $\frac{1}{4}$ of an inch on each piece. For seams attached to the zipper, there is $\frac{3}{8}$ of an inch. If there are 2 seams attached to the zipper, how much total fabric width is inside the seams on the bodice? _____

7. Kelly makes a mistake and needs to buy more fabric. If $\frac{3}{8}$ of a yard of fabric is $1.89, how much is the price per yard? _____

8. The dress is finally complete and Kelly is ready to leave, but now it's only 10 minutes before the dance is supposed to start at 8 PM! If Kelly's date drives at an average rate of 35 mph and the school is $12\frac{1}{2}$ miles away, about what time will they arrive? _____

Running in Circles

Using the measurements given, calculate the area of each of these items to the nearest hundredth.

1.

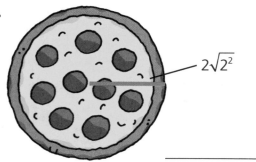

$2\sqrt{2^2}$

_____

2.

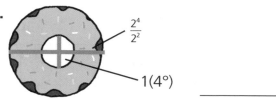

$\dfrac{2^4}{2^2}$

$1(4°)$

_____

3.

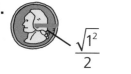

$\dfrac{\sqrt{1^2}}{2}$

_____

4.

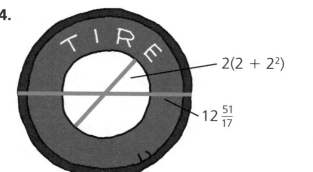

$2(2 + 2^2)$

$12\dfrac{51}{17}$

_____

5.

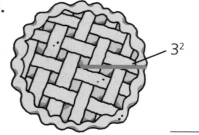

3^2

_____

6.

$|-5|$

_____

7.

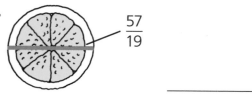

$\dfrac{57}{19}$

_____

8.

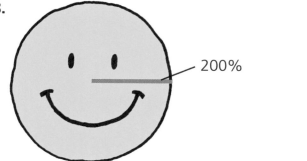

200%

_____

How Does Your Garden Grow?

The Kearney family is making a series of gardens in their yard. Each member of the family is digging his or her own garden. Erik Kearney has already dug his garden. It is labeled DEFG in the graph below. Use the information provided to determine the location of each person's garden.

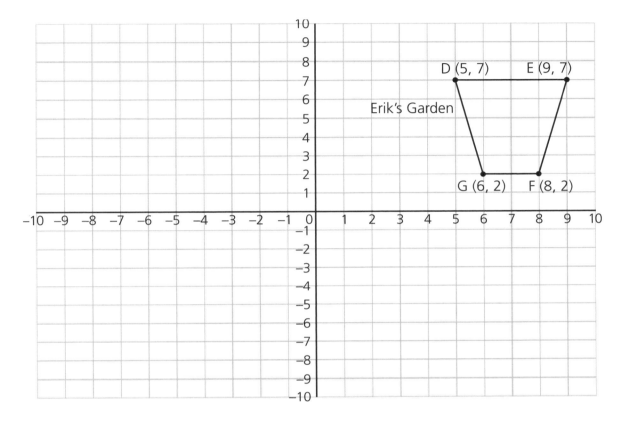

1. Matthew Kearney's garden is a reflection of Erik's garden across the *x*-axis. Draw it and label it MNOP. Write his name inside the garden.

2. Mark Kearney's garden is shaped like a right triangle. The right angle of Mark's garden is 4 units to the left of vertex G in Erik's garden. Vertex A of Mark's garden is 5 units higher than the right angle contained within it. Vertex B of Mark's garden is 3 units to the right of the right angle contained within it. Draw it and label it ABC. Write Mark's name inside the garden.

3. Danielle Kearney's garden is a reflection of Mark's garden across the *y*-axis. Draw it and label it JKL. Write her name inside the garden.

4. Richard Kearney's garden is a translation of Mark's garden and is 6 units to the left and 9 units down. Draw it and label it XYZ. Write his name inside the garden.

Sudoku Scramble

Each Sudoku puzzle has a unique solution that can be reached logically. Enter digits 1 to 9 into the blank spaces. Every row must contain one of each digit. So must every column, as must every 3 × 3 square. Complete these Sudoku puzzles as quickly as you can!

1.

	5	1	2				9	
	3	8		7	9		4	
2	9		5					6
1	2	3	6			7		
8	7		3		1		5	4
		9			8	3	6	1
4					2		1	5
	1		8	6		4	3	
	6				7	9	2	

2.

			6	4				7
			9	7	1		3	2
1			2		3	5		
5	1			6		7	9	8
			5		9			
9	6	4		3			2	5
		1	8		6			4
3	5		1	9	4			
6				5	7			

3.

	2	3		1		5		
5			8	2			6	
							3	
	7	6	4	5				3
	5	8	1		6	2	9	
1				9	8	6	5	
	3							
	1			8	9			6
		7		3		1	2	

4.

		1			4			2
	5				3		1	9
4	7							5
				8		2		7
		4		9		8		
8		6		3				
2							6	8
1	8		2				4	
5			3			9		

G'day Mate!

Charlie lives in San Francisco and is taking a December vacation to visit friends in Australia.
Help him make plans by solving the following problems.

1. Compute the total taxes and fees for each of Charlie's flight options and fill in the chart.

Airline	One-Way Price	Round-Trip Price	Taxes and Fees	Total
Boomerang	$959.40			$2,291.30
Transworld	$1,520.50			$3,422.30
Union Air	$1,936.50			$4,242.90
Kanga Lines	$639.00			$1,659.30

2. Which airline should Charlie choose based on price? _____

3. Right now, it is 9 PM on Saturday in San Francisco. It is 2 PM on Sunday in Sydney. What is the
time difference between San Francisco and Sydney? _____

4. Charlie knows how long his flight will take, but he wants to know what the local time will be
in Sydney when he arrives. Charlie's flight leaves at 11 PM on Sunday and flies west for 14 hours
and 25 minutes. What day and time will it be in Sydney when he arrives?

_____

5. Charlie booked a hotel in Sydney for 5 nights. The total price of his stay is AU$2,175 (Australian
dollars). If the exchange rate of AUD to U.S. dollars is 0.917, how much will it cost per night in
U.S. dollars? _____

Finally, Charlie arrives in Sydney. He hails a taxi at the airport to take him to his hotel.
The prices are posted on the back of the driver's seat. (Note: prices are in AUD.)

SYDNEY URBAN AREA FARES	
Flag Fall	$3.10
Distance Rate	$1.85 per kilometer
Waiting Time	$0.80 per minute when vehicle is traveling less than 26 km/hr
Tolls	All bridge, ferry, tunnel, and road tolls additional

6. The distance from the airport to Hotel Oasis is 18.75 kilometers. On the trip, they cross the Sydney Harbour Tunnel and pay tolls of AU$5.00. They get stuck in a traffic jam for 12.5 minutes. Charlie gives the driver a tip of 20%. What is the total price of Charlie's trip converted into U.S. dollars? _____

7. After spending 5 days in Sydney, Charlie is renting a car to visit his family, who live north of Sydney. He gets a rate of AU$59.00 per day for a 5-day rental car. His daily mileage allowance is 50 km. The charge for every kilometer above the total limit is AU$0.39. At the end of the rental, his total mileage is 368 km. Charlie also has a gas charge of 13 liters @ AU$1.49 a liter. How much is the total cost of the car rental converted into U.S. dollars? _____

8. Charlie's last night in Sydney is New Year's Eve. He and his cousins join the celebrations in Sydney Harbour. Charlie decides to call friends in San Francisco at midnight in Sydney to wish them a Happy New Year. What time is it in San Francisco? _____

Word Problem Whiz

Answer the questions below.

1. Anthony has 3 classes before lunch. If classes are the same length, and he has 3 minutes in between each class, how long are his classes if his morning lasts 2 hours and 39 minutes?

_____

2. Taj walked $2\frac{1}{4}$ miles to the hardware store. Then he walked *n* miles to the library. He was walking at a rate of 12 miles per hour and walked for a total of 36 minutes. What is the value of *n*?

_____

3. Lola had 9 gallons of paint. She used $1\frac{1}{4}$ gallons in the dining room, and $2\frac{1}{2}$ gallons in the kitchen. Lola used twice as much paint in the living room as the office. Lola used half as much paint in the office as she did in the kitchen. How much paint is left? _____

4. Kate is 63 inches tall. Greta is 68 inches tall. Rae is taller than Greta. Addison is two inches shorter than Greta. Amy is 1 inch shorter than Addison. The difference between Amy and Greta's height is the same as the difference between Greta and Rae's height. How tall is Rae?

_____

5. Elijiah and Ethan went to the movies. Tickets cost $9.75 each. Elijiah bought a small popcorn and a bottle of water. Ethan bought a box of candy. The water and candy cost the same amount. The small popcorn cost $5.50. If the friends spent a total of $30, how much were the water and candy? _____

6. Emmitt and Andy are selling wrapping paper for a band fund-raiser. Their goal is to sell $40 of wrapping paper each. Emmitt has sold twice as much wrapping paper as Andy so far. They have reached 75% of their combined goal. How many dollars worth of wrapping paper has Andy sold? _____

7. Monroe Middle School offers 4 languages to sixth graders: Spanish, French, German, and Mandarin Chinese. Twice as many students take Spanish as French. Of the total students, $\frac{1}{8}$ take Mandarin Chinese and 38 students take German. There are 256 students in the sixth grade. How many students study French? _____

8. Kyle is going to guess Logan's and Kwan's birthdays. He guesses September 16 for both of them. What is the probability that he has guessed one of their birthdays correctly if they were both born in a leap year? _____

9. There are 5 students in the Math League: Kyle, Emmitt, Ethan, Lola, and Greta. If each of these people shakes hands with every other person 1 time, how many total handshakes happen?

_____

10. The Math League has been posed with a challenge: write a math equation that contains 4 number 9s and equals 100. Write it here.

_____

Waste Not, Want Not

Use your knowledge of geometry to answer the questions below. Round your answers to the nearest tenth.

1. Holly got a square tablecloth as a gift. She is cutting it into a circular tablecloth with the pattern below. If 1 side of the square tablecloth is 2 yards long, how many square feet will the circular cloth be?

_____

2. Holly also received a set of napkins. They measure 10 inches diagonally. How many square inches is one napkin?

_____

2 yards

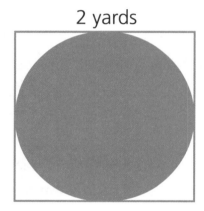

3. Julius wants to cut the largest possible square tabletop from a round piece of wood. What would be the measurement of 1 side of the new tabletop? _____

4. Ben is making a birdhouse and is cutting parts for the roof, which are shaded in on the diagram. If he uses this template for the pieces, what percentage of the piece is wasted? _____

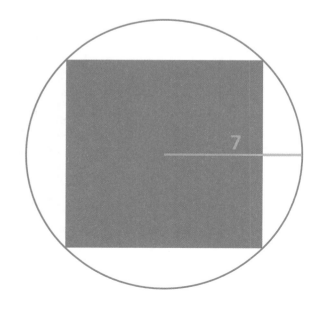

7

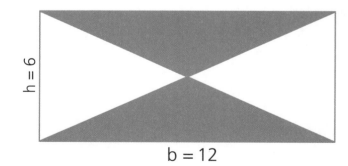

h = 6

b = 12

5. Suzie wants to make a pencil cup for her mom using a soup can and some wallpaper to re-cover the outside. The diameter of the can across the top is 4 inches. How long does the wallpaper piece need to be to wrap around the outside of the can exactly once with no overlap? _____

6. Art wants to make a tunnel for his pet gerbil. He has a piece of wood that is 6 × 4 × 3. If the tunnel cutout is half the width, two-thirds of the height, and cut all the way through the length, what proportion of the piece of wood is being cut away? _____

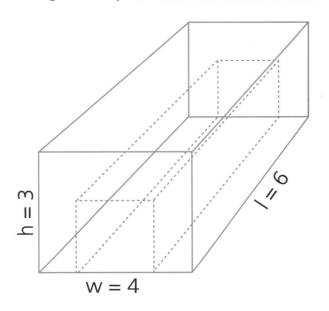

7. Betty is baking a special 10th birthday cake for her friend. She found the template below in a magazine. According to the instructions, the hole of the 0 should be $\frac{1}{3}$ of the width of the circle it is being cut from. If her cake pan is 9 × 12 inches, what percentage of the cake will be discarded after the 10 is cut out? _____

Answer Key

Page 4
1. 65,500,000
2. 208,000,000
3. 248,000,000
4. 145,500,000
5. 130,000
6. 4,600,000,000
7. 3,800,000,000
8. 2,500,000,000
9. 4,600,000,000
10. 443,000,000
11. 1,800,000
12. 360,000,000

Page 5
1. =
2. ≠
3. =
4. ≠
5. ≠
6. =
7. ≠
8. =
9. ≠
10. ≠
11. ≠
12. =

Page 6
1. 20
2. 48
3. 42
4. 18
5. 95
6. 6
7. 4
8. 12
9. 17
10. 12
11. 11
12. 9

Page 7
1. 1,568,744.3
2. 1,302,612.1
3. 19,799.98
4. −11,155.1
5. 2,470.09
6. 0.0529
7. 19.7136
8. 36,519.21
9. 17.4685
10. 25.53
11. 7.245
12. 575.115

Pages 8–9
1. 44
2. 10
3. 24
4. 12
5. 56
6. 78
7. 66
8. 40
9. 12
10. 51
11. 38
12. 81

Page 10
1. 1:7
2. 2:7
3. 4:7
4. 5:7
5. 3:5
6. 3:5
7. 1:4
8. 1:1

Page 11
1. acute
2. acute
3. obtuse
4. right
5. straight
6. obtuse
7. acute
8. obtuse
9. obtuse
10. acute
11. 40°, 60°, 80°
12. 30°, 60°, 90°

Page 12
1. −3,932
2. −66
3. −3,680
4. −684
5. 728,247
6. 198
7. −232
8. n = −8
9. n = −7
10. $-\frac{3}{20}$
11. $\frac{4}{9}$
12. 75.25

Page 13
1. $6.00
2. $3.40
3. $0.75
4. $0.25
5. $0.64
6. $9.00
7. $0.50
8. $1.45
9. $2.72
10. $3.45
11. $1.20
12. $29.36

Page 14
The following answers are circled:
1. $\frac{43}{172}$
2. 4:48
3. 390
4. $\frac{1}{12}$ gallon
5. 64
6. 10.5
7. 108
8. 3:4
9. 45 cm
10. $\frac{20}{8}$
11. $9\frac{3}{4}$
12. $\frac{1}{5}$ yard

Page 15
1. Answers will vary.
2. Answers will vary.
3. Answers will vary.

Page 16
1. $\frac{3}{5}$; 3:5
2. $\frac{1}{8}$; 1 to 8
3. 2 to 7; 2:7
4. 5 to 9; 5:9
5. $\frac{6}{5}$; 6 to 5
6. $\frac{3}{11}$; 3:11
7. $\frac{1}{8}$
8. $\frac{1}{3}$
9. $\frac{1}{9}$
10. $\frac{x}{y}$
11. $\frac{n}{1} = n$
12. $\frac{7}{2}$

Page 17
1. c
2. a
3. c
4. a
5. b
6. a
7. c
8. b

Page 18
1. 2%
2. 5%
3. 14%
4. 8%
5. 25%
6. 17%
7. 17%
8. 33%

Page 19
1.

59 people have dogs only.
2.

28 zoos have tigers only.

Page 20
1. 14.4 meters per second
2. 31 miles per hour
3. 1:44.2 or 1 minute and 44.2 seconds
4. 37.45 seconds
5. 13.4 meters per second
6. Cole
7. 33.78 seconds
8. 33.33 seconds

Page 21
1. e
2. i
3. g
4. b
5. k
6. a
7. c
8. l
9. d
10. j
11. f
12. h

Page 22
1. $122,346,000
2. $5,266.56
3. Hero Hank
   Tara's Sister
   Princess Lake
   My Day
   One Mistake
4. 2.6 weeks
5. $78,977,400
6. $74,854,000
7. It didn't make any money because it had not opened yet.
8. $132,243,600

Page 23
1. a lawyer
2. a doctor
3. a writer
4. an engineer

Pages 24–25
1.
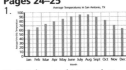
2. October and November
3. July and August
4.
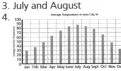
5. October and November
6. July and August
7. June and July
8. January

Page 26
1. 21%
2. 14%
3. 13%
4. 36%
5. 85%
6. 40%
7. 13
8. judgment

Page 27
1. 7°F
2. 5°F
3. −8°F
4. 9°F
5. −6°F
6. 10°F
7. (number line image)
8. none

Pages 28–29
1. 800
2. 14,000
3. 20,000,000
4. 20
5. 1,000
6. 300,000
7. 0.7
8. 2
9. $7
10. 120
11. $52
12. $86
13. $360
14. 280
15. $32
16. 600

Page 30
1. $8.40
2. $1.20
3. $9.75
4. selling 14 slices
5. 7 pies
6. 5 brownies
7. 5 slices of apple pie
8. $4.13

Page 31
1. 4 s'mores
2. $5\frac{1}{4}$ cups of chili
3. 8 pancakes
4. 57 ounces
5. $5\frac{1}{2}$ packages
6. $3\frac{1}{2}$ cups

Page 32
1. 26.75 field goals
2. 26.5 field goals
3. 24 field goals
4. 4.25 field goals
5. kicker 6
6. kicker 8
7. 240 points
8. 46 extra point kicks made

Page 33
1. 3,125 sq. ft.
2. 417,720 sq. ft.
3. 41,154 sq. ft.
4. 14,400 sq. ft.
5. 819,975 sq. ft.
6. 35,547 sq. ft.
7. 48,735 sq. ft.
8. 4,374 sq. ft.

Page 34
1. 23
2. 12
3. 12
4. Caitlyn sent many more text messages than her friends. Her 159 text messages make the average higher than it would have been if she were not part of Serena's poll. The median is not affected by Caitlin's high number of text messages, so it gives Serena a better idea of how many messages her friends usually send.
5. 9.3
6. 6.5
7. 32.3
8. 11.2

Page 35
1. 0.282
2. night games
3. 0.289
4. 63
5. 22%
6. He should play the afternoon game. Better has a higher batting average during day games than during night games, so there is a higher probability that Better will have a hit in the day game.
7. 0.298
8. 6%

Pages 36–37
1. 59.69 mm
2. 283.53 mm
3. 80 pennies
4. 1,000 pennies
5. 65.97 mm
6. 346.36 mm
7. 17 nickels
8. 475 grams
9. 56.55 mm
10. 254.47 mm
11. 75 dimes
12. $15.00
13. $3.25
14. 24.26 mm
15. 76.21 mm
16. 462.23 mm

Page 38
1. The correct shape is a rhombus with sides of 4 inches.
2. rhombus
3. The correct shape is a rectangle with two sides of 2 inches and two sides of 3 inches.
4. rectangle
5. The correct shape is a square with sides of 4 inches.

6. square
7. The correct shape is a trapezoid with parallel lines for the top and bottom. The sides are drawn as follows: the top is 6 inches; the bottom is 11 inches; the left side is 5.9 inches; the right side is 5.9 inches.
8. trapezoid

Page 39
1. b
2. d
3. a
4. b

Page 40
1. $32.40
2. $15
3. $64
4. $49.30
5. $72
6. $75
7. $60
8. $36.90

Page 41
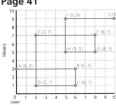
1. 41 m
2. 25 ft

Page 42
1. 24
2. 102
3. 10
4. 3
5. 312
6. 4.26
7. 7.5
8. 546
9. 1
10. 7
11. 0.2
12. 1.2
SURFIN' SAFARI

Page 43
1. $23.85
2. $19.55
3. $19.15
4. $0.80
5. 8
6. 58 books
7. $17.98
8. 8 hours

Page 44
1. b
2. d
3. b
4. a
5. b
6. d
7. b
8. c

Page 45
1. Jacob must take the bunny across to safety and leave it on the other side of the river. On the next trip, Jacob must take his dingo to safety and leave it on the other side of the river, but he must return to the farm with his bunny in the rowboat. On his next trip, Jacob must leave his bunny at the farm, but take his carrots to safety and leave it on the other side of the river. On his next trip, Jacob must get his bunny from the farm and finally, all will be on the other side of the river.
2. 7 one-way trips

Page 46
1. 12
2. 24
3. $70.50
4. 18
5. 10
6. $\frac{2}{3}$
7. 8

Page 47
1. 33°
2. 62°
3. 1°
4. 73°
5. 27°
6. 45°
7. 70°
8. 144°
9. 115°
10. 90°
11. 10°
12. 55°

Pages 48–49
Recipe cards should read as follows:

APPLESAUCE
2 pints apples, peeled, cored, and cut into thick slices
$\frac{3}{16}$ cups water
$\frac{1}{4}$ pints brown sugar
4 tablespoons lemon juice
$\frac{1}{12}$ tablespoon nutmeg
1 teaspoon cinnamon
6 teaspoons butter

Place the peeled, cored, and diced apples in a saucepan. Add water, brown sugar, lemon juice, nutmeg, and cinnamon. Cover and cook over medium-low heat until apples are tender. This takes $\frac{1}{3}$–$\frac{1}{2}$ hours. Remove cover and cook for an additional 300 seconds to allow some of the moisture to evaporate. Stir in butter. Serve warm or cold.

PORCUPINE MEATBALLS
8 ounces ground beef
$\frac{1}{2}$ pound ground pork
$\frac{1}{2}$ pint onion, chopped
3 tablespoons butter
12 teaspoons rice
3 1-cup cans tomato sauce
$\frac{1}{6}$ quart water
$\frac{1}{4}$ teaspoon parsley flakes
$\frac{1}{16}$ pound bacon, cut into small pieces
Salt and pepper to taste

Preheat oven to 163°C. Mix beef and pork together. Add salt, pepper, and rice. Sauté onion in butter. Cool. Add to meat mixture. Form into meatballs. Mix tomato sauce and water in a bowl. Pour over meatballs. Sprinkle with parsley flakes. Top with bacon pieces. Cook covered for 1$\frac{1}{4}$ hours at 325°F. Let stand 15 minutes before serving.

Page 50
1. Micah bought a hockey helmet. Zoey bought hockey gloves and a hockey stick. Avery bought a hockey stick and a pack of hockey pucks.
2. Micah spent $40. Avery spent $46.50. Zoey spent $40.50.

Page 51
1. I
2. C
3. L
4. H
5. D
6. G
7. B
8. F
9. A
10. K
11. J
12. E

Pages 52–53
Answers will vary.

Page 54
1. 440 bills
2. 264,000,000 bills
3. $14,540.00
4. About 1,067 bills
5. $3,680,000.00
6. Answers will vary.
7. Answers will vary.
8. Answers will vary.

Page 55
1. 5,184 cubic inches
2. 9 cubic inches
3. 729 cubic inches
4. 45 cubic inches
5. 1,000 cubic inches
6. 160 cubic inches
7. 4 cubic inches
8. 7,680 cubic inches
9. Box #2 or #7
10. Box #8

Page 56

Candidate	Percent of Votes as a Decimal	Number of Votes
Kannry	0.30	10,200
Denega	0.20	6,800
Quigley	0.17	5,780
Allgood	0.08	2,720
Woods	0.05	1,700
Weiss	0.01	340
Hill	0.03	1,020
McCartney	0.06	2,040
Bright	0.10	3,400
Total	1.00	34,000

1. Candidate Kannry
2. 3,400 votes
3. 3,778
4. It is the low end of the range, so Weiss brings the mean down to a lower number. If Weiss was eliminated, the mean would be higher, at 4,208 votes.

Page 57
1. $3.32
2. $8.56
3. $2.12
4. $17.98
5. $5.70
6. $3.14
7. $9.28
8. $8.08
9. $7.50
10. $8.00
11. $36.40
12. $9.40

Page 58
1. 313,617
2. 235,422
3. 546,888
4. 27%
5. 2,821,920
6.

Year	Population
(graph showing population increasing from 2,000,000 in 2000 to 2,600,000 in 2007)

7. 2003–2004
8. 2002–2003

Page 59
Problems 1–6 are correct when triangles with these characteristics are drawn:
1. a triangle with all sides different lengths
2. a triangle that contains one right angle and has two sides that are equal in length
3. a triangle with all sides the same length
4. a triangle that has one angle that is greater than 90°
5. a triangle in which all three angles are less than 90°
6. a triangle with two sides that are the same length and no right angles
7. no
8. 53° and 90°

Page 60
1. 15$\frac{1}{6}$
2. 10$\frac{1}{4}$
3. $0.14
4. 25$\frac{7}{12}$
5. 5
6. 12$\frac{1}{4}$
7. 7$\frac{1}{2}$
8. 10$\frac{1}{9}$

Page 61
1. 3; 6; 8
2. 36 ounces = 2$\frac{1}{4}$ pounds OR 48 ounces = 3 pounds
3,000 milligrams = 3 grams OR 3 milligrams = 0.003 grams
1 quart = 4 cups OR $\frac{1}{2}$ quart = 2 cups

Page 62
1. 90 inches
2. 24 sq. ft.
3. 68.25 sq. ft.
4. 126 inches
5. 36.75 sq. ft.

Page 63
1. 5,999,999,999
2. 7,625,431
3. 95,876
4. 799,899,999,999
5. 65,324
6. 487,563

Page 64
1. 40 feet
2. 251.2 feet
3. 5,024 sq. ft.
4. 20,000 sq. ft.
5. 14,976 sq. ft.

Page 65
1. $\frac{3}{16}$
2. $-\frac{3}{7}$

3. $-\frac{79}{729}$
4. $\frac{1}{16}$
5. $\frac{25}{72}$
6. 2$\frac{1}{2}$ inches
7. $\frac{3}{8}$ sq. in.
8. 73 days
9. 54
10. 8 ounces

Page 66
1. 52.5 minutes
2. 1.6 hours
3. 72 minutes
4. 7.5 miles
5. 440 miles
6. 594 kilometers
7. Car B
8. Angel

Page 67
Answers will vary.

Page 68
1. 2
2. They ate the same amount.
3. 29%
4. $8.74
5. $2.31
6. 6 large meatball pizzas
7. 21
8. 10

Page 69
1. $500.00
2. $2,500.00
3. 72 months
4. $16,500.00
5. $432.29
6. $5,000.00
7. $19,000
8. $375.00
9. Answers will vary, but should indicate a clear opinion based on price, technology (like Sport or Hybrid), size, or fuel efficiency.

Page 70
1. 100°
2. 50°
3. 130°
4. 30°
5. 90°
6. 50°

Page 71
1. yes
2. yes
3. no
4. yes
5. yes
6. no
7. no
8. yes

Pages 72–73
1. 10:99
2. 19:99
3. 1:12
4. 7:23
5. 1:5
6. 9
7. 19:20
8. 1:12
9. 11
10. 7:5
11. 51:50
12. 11:19

Page 74
1. 20%
2. 60%
3. 56%
4. 4,020 miles
5. 260 miles
6. 1,372,800 feet

7. 2,822 miles
8. 3,079 miles

Page 75
1. −0.60
2. 0.67
3. 0.56
4. 1.86
5. −1.25
6. 1.38
7. −0.17
8. −0.29
9. 0.83
10. 0.16
11. 0.01
12. 0.48

(number line graphic)

Page 76
1. 98%
2. 1½ teaspoons
3. 15 milliliters
4. 200 teaspoons
5. 13%
6. 120/80
7. 2%
8. 5 hours

Page 77
1. 262.5 knee bangs
2. 105 minutes or 1 hour, 45 minutes
3. 48 players
4. 392 men
5. 7 neck injuries
6. 264 times
7. $2,250.00
8. 98 members

Page 78
1. 86,822 miles
2. 7,918 miles
3. 1,516 miles
4. 3,485.4 miles
5. 2,106 miles
6. 1,118 miles per hour
7. 57°F
8. false

Page 79
1. 77,696 sq. ft.
2. 34,963 sq. ft.
3. 9,712 sq. ft.
4. none
5. 50%
6. 57,600 sq. ft.

Pages 80–81
Answers will vary.

Pages 82–83
1. $19.90
2. $15.75
3. $12.30
4. $21.56
5. no
6. 13
7. $\frac{5}{8}$
8. $\frac{1}{4}$ lb of each
9. $7.88
10. $7.90
11. $2.00
12. $8.20

Page 84
1. 10.7
2. 10.5
3. 9
4. 10.8

Page 85
1. yes
2. yes
3. yes
4. no
5. 240°
6. 102°
7. 156°
8. 36°

Page 86
1. 4
2. c
3. Yes. With 40% of voters undecided, she would need to secure 26% of those in order to win the election.
4. 5%
5. $75.50
6. $0.19

Page 87
1. 35.33 cubic feet
2. 12.56 cubic feet
3. 42.39 cubic feet
4. 31.79 cubic feet
5. 0.79 cubic feet
6. 226.08 cubic feet
7. 19.63 cubic feet
8. 26.98 cubic feet
9. yes
10. Barrel #6

Page 88
1. (F − 32) ÷ $\frac{9}{5}$
2. France
3. Greece
4. England
5. Norway
6. Italy
7. It is farther north than the others.
8. France and England

Page 89
1. B
2. 87%
3. B
4. 90%
5. C
6. 93%
7. D
8. 90%

Page 90
1. White Plains; 95; Redding
2. Harrison; 77
3. 81; Mount Kisco
4. Chappaqua; 99; Westport

Page 91
1. translation
2. integers
3. variable
4. reflection
5. absolute value
6. origin
7. function
8. inequality

Pages 92–93
1. 4 feet per minute
2. $119.08
3. 8%
4. 48 shells
5. 857 minutes
6. 63 ants
7. 6 meters
8. 528 peppers

Page 94
1. Virginia
2. Virginia: 8
Ohio: 7
Massachusetts: 4
New York: 4
North Carolina: 2
Texas: 2
Vermont: 2
3. (bar graph)
4. 4.1
5. 4

Page 95
1. 0.44
2. 4.41
3. 6.39
4. 1.10
5. 2.64
6. 6.61
7. 2.87
8. 5.00
9. 3.86
10. 1.65

Pages 96–97
Races 1 and 2
1. 3
2. 12
3. 5,280
4. 2.2
5. 16
6. 2,000
7. 0.01
8. 1,000,000
9. 8
10. 2
11. 2
12. 4

Page 98
1. 1 hour, 1 minute
2. $6.93
3. 17%
4. Track 5
5. 4:55
6. 4:55
7. 3:24
8. 5:05
9. Track 1 is much longer that the other songs, so it's making the mean higher.
10. Track 8 is much shorter than the other songs, so it's making the mean lower.

Page 99
1. 4,700 sq. ft.
2. 79
3. by the gallon
4. $700.00
5. 560
6. 288 feet
7. 54%
8. this season

Page 100
1. 5 gallons
2. 112 miles
3. 5 gallons
4. 58%
5. 472.5 miles
6. 107.25 miles
7. $66.99
8. 12.25 gallons

Page 101
1. (bar graph)
2. 16,270.916 feet
3. 15,932 feet
4. Alaska

Page 102
1. 28%
2. 55%
3. $\frac{1}{2}$
4. 42.9%
5. 12%
6. 3.3 bags

Page 103
1. 7
2. 2
3. 3
4. 2
5. 4
6. 9
7. 5
8. 8
9. 18
10. 18
Puzzle Answer:
SHE HAD BUZZ

Page 104
1. 13 days
2. 11 days
3. 10 days
4. 11 days
5. 6,072,000 feet
6. 71.875 miles
7. 1.2%
8. 1,140 dogs

Page 105
2. Answers will vary.
3. Answers will vary.
4. Answers will vary.
5. Answers will vary.

Page 106
1. 180
2. 18
3. 17
4. 17
5. 18
6. Kevin and Jamina
7. $120.00
8. 10

Page 107
1. The plastic pitcher was $\frac{7}{8}$ full of sweet tea.
2. The glass was $\frac{6}{6}$ full, or completely full, of fruit punch.

Pages 108–109
1. Cougars
2. Panthers
3. The Cheetahs scored more runs and allowed fewer runs than the Tigers.
4. Tigers
5. Panthers
6. 96%
7. 92%
8. 83%
9. 66%
10. 57%
11. 11%
12. 31.5 runs

Page 110
1. January
2. June and July
3. 89°F
4. 92.5°F
5. 103°F
6. 33°
7. Aswan
8. (bar graph)

Page 111
1. 2 lb. of potatoes; 1½ lb. of ground beef; 1⅓ cups of carrots
2. 18

Page 112
1. 648 feet
2. 39.4 meters
3. 60 feet
4. 96 meters
5. 81.6 meters
6. 97.6 feet
7. 112.4 feet
8. 2 miles

Page 113
1. b
2. a
3. a
4. b
5. a
6. b
7. b
8. b

Page 114
1. 7:400
2. 3:800
3. 1:40
4. 1:80
5. 1:36
6. 3:103
7. 1:9

Page 115
1. no, 1,352
2. no, 1,400 feet
3. yes
4. no, 111 pounds
5. yes
6. no, $\frac{7}{6}$

Page 116
1. 78
2. 42
3. 21
4. 0
5. There is not enough information provided to answer this question.
6. 14
7. 47
8.

Page 117
1. a
2. c
3. c
4. b
5. a
6. b
7. c
8. a

Page 118
Answers will vary.

Page 119
1. 4
2. 1
3. 18
4. 12
5. 1.333
6. 0
7. 0
8. 0.5

Page 120
1. ostrich
2. 1 inch; 6.28 inches
3. 0.318 kilogram
4. 18 seconds
5. 264,000 feet
6. 3.3 feet
7. 9 feet
8. 1,400%

Page 121
1. Jaclyn filled 6 bags.
   Shareef filled 7 bags. Susie
   filled 5 bags.
   Chris filled 6 bags.
2. Jaclyn had 8 bottles in
   each bag.
   Shareef had 6 bottles in
   each bag.
   Susie had 9 bottles in
   each bag.
   Chris had 7 bottles in
   each bag.
3. Jaclyn and Shareef

Page 122
1. apples
2. peaches
3. 28
4. 12
5. 24
6.

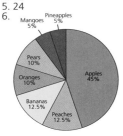

7. 225
8. 225

Page 123
1. 6 ounces
2. 14 pounds, 3 ounces
3. 2 feet
4. 13 yards, 1 foot
5. 1 foot, 7 inches
6. 20 feet, 2 inches
7. 21 centimeters
8. 12 centimeters,
   1 millimeter
9. 4 tons, 930 pounds
10. 9 grams, 50 milligrams
11. 1 cup
12. 6 gallons, 1 quart

Pages 124–125
1. 2 hours, 7$\frac{1}{2}$ minutes
2. $13.18
3. $8.27
4. $13.95
5.

INVOICE				
Mr. Al Lowry
33 Sunshine Street
Lawn Mowing	2.125 Hours	x	$6.20	= $13.18
Edge Trimming	1.33 Hours	x	$6.20	= $8.27
Gutter Cleaning	1.5 Hours	x	$9.30	= $13.95
			GRAND TOTAL:	$ 35.40

6. 14
7. $42.14
8. $517.82
9. $1.75
10. C = $10 + $\frac{m}{250}$

Page 126

	Adventure	Party Animal	Brainpower Test	Brainbuster	Holiday
Anna			YES		
Ian	YES				
David		YES			
Carly				YES	
Nick					YES

1. Nick
2. Carly
3. David
4. Ian
5. Anna

Page 127
1. 28 miles
2. 5 miles
3. 7:48 AM
4. 4:24 PM
5. 6 mph
6. Dory
7. 13 gallons
8. 2 hours, 14 minutes

Page 128
1. 85 points
2. 16 points
3. 75%
4. 12.5%
5. 116 points
6. 152 points
7. Team A
8. Team H

Page 129
1. 1,024 cubic inches
2. 660 cubic inches
3. 2,016 cubic inches
4. 2,160 cubic inches
5. 864 cubic inches
6. 855 cubic inches
7. 4 cubic feet
8. $59.97

Page 130
1. B
2. E
3. C
4. 324 centimeters
5. 50.24 inches
6. C and D
7. A
8. D

Page 131
1. USA: 95.439 seconds
   Australia: 95.675 seconds
   Germany: 95.7 seconds
   Zimbabwe: 96.49 seconds
2. USA: gold
   Australia: silver
   Germany: bronze
   Zimbabwe: no medal

Page 132
1. 14
2. 5 hours, 50 minutes
3. 2.3 minutes
4. $484.29
5. 7 weeks
6. Answers will vary. He will
   have to work fewer hours
   as a dishwasher. But, he
   will earn less per hour as
   a dishwasher.

Page 133
1. 18 inches
2. 7 inches
3. 18 centimeters
4. 24 inches
5. 16 centimeters
6. 42 centimeters
7. 27 inches
8. 20 centimeters

Page 134
1. 1,800 points
2. Ben needs to perform 60
   zero gravity jumps
   (60 × 10 = 600 points),
   24 moon rock climbs
   (24 × 25 = 600 points),
   and 6 flag plants
   (6 × 100 = 600 points).
3. Ben needs to perform 4
   flag plants (4 × 100 =
   400 points), 32 moon
   rock climbs (32 × 25 =
   800 points), and 40 zero
   gravity jumps (40 × 10 =
   400 points).
4. No

Page 135
1. 20.48
2. 16.60
3. 30.81
4. 178.59
5. 85
6. 45.5
7. 64.6
8. 12.5
9. trapezoids
10. 10 × 10

Pages 136–137
1. b
2. d
3. d
4. b
5. a
6. b
7. d
8. b

Page 138
Answers will vary.

Page 139
1. 24 (6 × 4)
2. 20 (4 × 5)
3. 2
4. 126 (7 × 6 × 3)
5. 210 (7 × 6 × 5)
6. $13.00

Page 140
1.
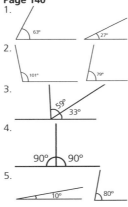
2.
3.
4.
5.
6.

Page 141
1. 1 cubic inch
2.

3. 28 cubic inches
4.
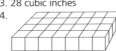
5. 84 cubic inches
6.
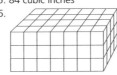
7. 84 cubic inches

8.
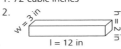

Page 142
1. b
2. b
3. a
4. two gallons
5. five pints
6. yes
7. b
8. a

Page 143
1. 3
2. Race 3 had the fastest
   average speed
   (158 mph).
3. 1,500 miles
4. 140 miles per hour
5. 133 miles per hour
6. 4.38 hours
7. 2.88 hours
8. Ace Putty

Page 144
1. 20 quarters, 50 dimes
2. Eagles; Eagles 18,
   Hornets 17
3. 3.25 pounds
4. $700.00
5. $350.00
6. $280.00

Page 145
1. 72 cubic inches
2.

3. 1,180 cubic centimeters
4. 480 cubic centimeters
5. 1,944 cubic centimeters
6. Box B

Page 146
Answers to questions 1–4
can be in any order:
(−5, 4) corresponds to (−2, 1)
(−3, 2) corresponds to (0, −1)
(−2, 7) corresponds to (1, 4)
(0, 5) corresponds to (3, 2)
5. Answers will vary.
6. Answers will vary.

Page 147
1. 7:17 PM
2. 10:47 AM
3. 11:51 PM
4. 3:26 PM
5. 12:45 AM
6. 1:42 AM
7. 4:18 PM
8. 5:01 PM
9. 6:20 PM
10. 12:36 PM

Page 148
1. 8%
2. 15%
3. 224,961 square miles
4. 124,502 square miles
5. 10,170 square miles

Page 149
1. 10
2. 8
3. 8
4. 18
5. 7
6. 4
7. 3
8. 3
9. 5
10. 12
11. 7
12. −3.5
Puzzle answer:
AT THE MOOVIES

Pages 150–151
1. 10.35 meters per second
2. 400 meters
3. 9.104 meters per second
4. 10%
5. 1,123
6. 21:22
7. 7
8.

	Nation	Gold	Silver	Bronze	Total
1	USA	304	229	182	715
2	Soviet Union	64	51	74	193
3	Great Britain	48	76	60	184
4	Finland	48	35	29	112
5	East Germany	38	36	35	109

9. Finland
10. Great Britain

Page 152
1. acute
2. acute
3. right
4. obtuse
5. obtuse
6. right
7. isosceles
8. scalene
9. equilateral
10. 30°
11. 72°
12. 51°

Page 153
1. 70.5 mph
2. Mark
3. 67.1 mph
4. 89.1 mph
5. 164.9 feet
6. 81.4 mph

Page 154
1. 12
2. 5
3. 3
4. 10
5. 5
6. 6
7. 14
8. 3
9. 85
10. 6
11. 16
12. 13
Puzzle answer:
THEY HAVE BARK

Page 155
1. Chicago
2. Boston
3. Shanghai
4. Dublin
5. Kiev
6. 77°F
7. 86°F
8. 72°F
9. 91°F
10. 95°F

Pages 156–157
1. 68 quarts
2. 4
3. 7
4. 3
5. 272 glasses
6. $11.97
7. $140.00

191

8. $18.60
9. Yes. After Laila and Leanne covered their expenses (cups and mix), they earned $109.43.
10. $207.50
11. 48 quarts
12. 192 glasses

Page 158
1. b
2. b
3. d
4. a
5. d
6. c
7.

x	y	(x, y)
−3	2	(−3, 2)
−1	4	(−1, 4)
0	5	(0, 5)
1	6	(1, 6)
2	7	(2, 7)
3	8	(3, 8)

8.

x	y	(x, y)
−5	−15	(−5, −15)
−3	−9	(−3, −9)
−1	−3	(−1, −3)
0	0	(0, 0)
2	6	(2, 6)
5	15	(5, 15)

Page 159
1. 65+ years old
2. 15–24 years old
3. 4,094
4. 2,136
5. The population of people ages 5–14 is nearly double that of people ages 15–24. Youngstown can likely expect that the number of high school students will increase over the next several years.
6. 2%
7. 4%
8. Answers may vary. One choice is to put the six age groups on the x-axis. Each age group gets its own bar. The y-axis would give the population count. At minimum, the y-axis should include numbers from 1,602 (population of 15–24 year-olds) to 4,094 (population of those 65 and older).

Page 160
1. $A = \pi r^2$
2. $d = 2r$
3. $A = \frac{1}{2}bh$
4. $A = s^2$
5. $V = lwh$
6. $P = l + w + l + w$ or $P = 2l + 2w$
7. $A = lw$
8. $A = \frac{1}{2}bh$
9. $C = 2\pi r$ or $C = \pi d$
10. $V = \frac{hB}{3}$
11. $A = bh$
12. $A = r^2h$
Personal times will vary.

Page 161
1. 2325.55
2. 11378.02
3. 0.42%
4. 2.23%
5. 124.59
6. 2953.68
7. 26%
8. 5%

Pages 162–163
1.

2.
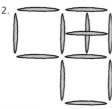
3. START HERE
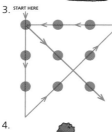
4.
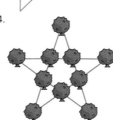

Page 164
1. $4^2 = 16$; $(3 \times 5) + 1 = 16$
2. $46^2 = 2,116$; $(45 \times 47) + 1 = 2,116$
3. $100^2 = 10,000$; $(99 \times 101) + 1 = 10,000$
4. The square of the middle number in the set = the product of the first number in the set multiplied by the third number in the set, plus one.
5.
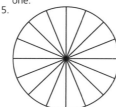
divide by two; multiply by $\frac{1}{2}$.
6.

divide by $\frac{1}{2}$; multiply by 2.

Page 165
1. $x \leq 3$
2. $x > -2$
3. $x \geq -1$
4. $x < 4$
5.
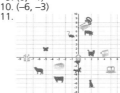
6.

Pages 166–167
1. (0, 7)
2. (−1, 5)
3. (−5, 2)
4. (2, 1)
5. (0, 7)
6. (0, −3)
7. (2, −6)
8. (−3, −5)
9. (0, −1)
10. (−6, −3)
11.
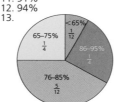

Pages 168–169
1. 79%
2. 80%
3. 91%
4. 67%
5. 64%
6. 69%
7. 83%
8. 74%
9. 82%
10. 79%
11. 91%
12. 94%
13.
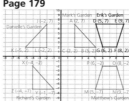
14. 79%
15. 79.5%
16. There are two modes: 79% and 91%
17. 30
18. Player 6
19. 79%
20. 73%

Pages 170–171
1. $6 + \frac{1}{3}n = n$; $n = 9$
2. $(40 + n) \div 2 = 48$; $n = 56$
3. $23 + 27 + 31 + 22 + n = 144$; $n = 41$
4. $(5 \times 28,342) − 2,588 = n$; $n = 139,122$
5. $n − $15.09 − $12.34 + $5.50 − $6.77 = 17.90; $n = 46.60$
6. $4n + n + 2n + 7 = 56$; $n = 7$; Ana has 28 markers; Adelaide has 7 markers; Miles has 14 markers; George has 7 markers
7. $36 − (36 \div 9) − 3 = n$; $n = 29$
8. $n[3(2 + 1 + 2 + 3)] = 166.80$; $n = 6.95

Page 172
1. 31 inches
2. 28 centimeters
3. 21 centimeters
4. 19 centimeters
5. 20.25 inches
6. 9.75, 7.5, and 3 inches
7. 45 inches
8. 24 inches

Page 173
1. 8 people; they are: 4 kids (2 boys and 2 girls), the mom and dad of those 4 kids, and the grandma and grandpa of the kids on the dad's side.
2. 66 km per day

Pages 174–175
1. plane
2. train
3. driving own car
4. $1.21
5. $15.09
6. $28.16
7. $257.00
8. $711.00
9. $230.00
10. $1,378.00

Pages 176–177
1. 94.5 inches
2. silk satin
3. 3
4. the gold belt
5. 6
6. $2\frac{3}{4}$ inches
7. $5.04
8. 8:11 PM

Page 178
1. 50.24
2. 11.78
3. 0.79
4. 63.61
5. 254.47
6. 78.5
7. 7.07
8. 12.56

Page 179

Pages 180–181
1.

7	5	1	2	4	6	8	9	3
6	3	8	1	7	9	5	4	2
2	9	4	5	8	3	1	7	6
1	2	3	6	5	4	7	8	9
8	7	6	3	9	1	2	5	4
5	4	9	7	2	8	3	6	1
4	8	7	9	3	2	6	1	5
9	1	2	8	6	5	4	3	7
3	6	5	4	1	7	9	2	8

2.

2	3	9	6	4	5	8	1	7
4	8	5	9	7	1	6	3	2
1	7	6	2	8	3	5	4	9
5	1	3	4	6	2	7	9	8
8	2	7	5	1	9	4	6	3
9	6	4	7	3	8	1	2	5
7	9	1	8	2	6	3	5	4
3	5	8	1	9	4	2	7	6
6	4	2	3	5	7	9	8	1

3.

6	2	3	9	1	7	5	4	8
5	9	4	8	2	3	7	6	1
7	8	1	6	4	5	9	3	2
9	7	6	4	5	2	8	1	3
3	5	8	1	7	6	2	9	4
1	4	2	3	9	8	6	5	7
2	3	9	7	6	1	4	8	5
4	1	5	2	8	9	3	7	6
8	6	7	5	3	4	1	2	9

4.

3	9	1	8	5	4	6	7	2
6	5	8	7	2	3	4	1	9
4	7	2	6	1	9	3	8	5
9	1	5	4	8	6	2	3	7
7	3	4	1	9	2	8	5	6
8	2	6	5	3	7	1	9	4
2	4	3	9	7	1	5	6	8
1	8	9	2	6	5	7	4	3
5	6	7	3	4	8	9	2	1

Pages 182–183
1.

Airline	One-Way Fare	Round-Trip Fare	Fees and Fuel	Total
Boomerang	$959.40	$1,918.80	$372.50	$2,291.30
Transworld	$1,520.50	$3,041.00	$381.30	$3,422.30
Union Air	$1,936.50	$3,873.00	$369.90	$4,242.90
Kanga Lines	$639.00	$1,278.00	$381.30	$1,659.30

2. Kanga Lines
3. Sydney is 17 hours ahead.
4. Tuesday, 6:25 AM
5. $398.90
6. $58.09
7. $330.48
8. 7 AM

Pages 184–185
1. 50 minutes
2. 4.95 miles
3. $1\frac{1}{2}$ gallons
4. 71 inches
5. $2.50 each
6. $20
7. 62
8. 1:183
9. 10
10. $99 + (9 \div 9) = 100$

Pages 186–187
1. 28.3 square feet
2. 50 square inches
3. 9.9
4. 50%
5. 12.6 inches
6. $\frac{1}{3}$
7. 22.7%

192